"This book is exactly what has been missi[ng] collection! It expands on the idea of Japa[nese] entertaining in the most easy-to-follow a[nd] to cook from it!"

—**Anita Lo**, chef and host, Tour de Forks tra[vel]

"A culinary plot twist: Aaron and Sawa have found true magic by bringing their two cultures together. Soulful, daring, and delicious; their food will satisfy cravings that you never even knew you had."

—**Zoë Kravitz**, actor and avid Shalom Japan fan

"Anyone who has been lucky enough to dine at Shalom Japan knows just how special Sawa and Aaron's food is. But this book offers a different, equally as delicious, and most practical treat: a glimpse into Sawa and Aaron's home life, where comforting and satisfying Japanese-influenced meals need to be eaten by the kids' bath times, and are occasionally prepped with an infant in arms. Between the hotpot tutorial, ketchup pasta (!!), and all of the tasty sandos, this book is sure to inspire cooks of all levels, no matter how familiar they are with Japanese cuisine."

—**Molly Yeh**, *New York Times* bestselling author and Food Network host

"In writing this book, Sawako and Aaron, along with Gabriella, demonstrate their passion to share their wonderful home-style dishes with a broad American cooking audience. The approach taken is to use readily available ingredients and cooking equipment found in U.S. home kitchens. The infectious joy of Sawako and Aaron and their family spills from the pages of this book, and cooks who prepare these dishes will provide health and happiness to their own families."

—**Hiroko Shimbo**, Japanese cuisine authority and chef instructor

LOVE
JAPAN

Recipes from Our
Japanese American Kitchen

Sawako Okochi & Aaron Israel

with Gabriella Gershenson

Photographs by Yuki Sugiura

TEN SPEED PRESS
California | New York

To Shuko Okochi
And to our children, Kaishu and Mayako

Contents

Basics

Breakfast

Vegetables

Pancakes and Friends

Sandos

Noodles

Hotpot and Tabletop Cooking

Fish

Poultry and Meat

Rice

Dessert

Gohan Desuyo! (Time to Eat!)

By Sawa and Aaron

At its core, this cookbook is a love story about how two chefs from different worlds fell for each other, and for each other's cuisines. We met in 2011 in New York City on a setup at a Chinese restaurant, which was soon followed by a procession of late-night dinners out, leisurely home-cooked breakfasts, and rooftop beers during the odd hours that chefs keep. Eventually we fell in love, moved in together, and decided to go all in and open our own restaurant, Shalom Japan, in Williamsburg, Brooklyn. It's a quirky, improbable project, a Japanese-Jewish restaurant that melds the foods of our roots, which for one of us is in Hiroshima, Japan, and for the other in a Jewish-American household on Long Island. To some, the concept may seem like a novelty, but for us, it's a reflection of the life we built together, one in which matzoh ball ramen and lox rice bowls are as commonplace as spaghetti and meatballs are in other families.

As important as the restaurant is to our lives and livelihood, this book isn't about that. It's about the food that we cook and eat in our Japanese American kitchen. When we started to build our life together, it became clear how much we were influenced by Sawa's mother's home cooking, which is as flavorful as it is nutritious, heavy on vegetables and fermented foods, with lots and lots of variety. (She'd always tell Sawa to eat thirty ingredients a day so she could get nutrition from varied sources.) We wanted to provide the same nourishment for our family, and to yours. Whether or not you have a Japanese parent (or in-law), we still want you to be able to experience the unique pleasure of digging into a heaping platter of golden karaage (fried chicken) or crispy, juicy harumaki (Japanese spring rolls). *Love Japan* is our way of sharing these meals that we cherish the most with you.

Our life together hasn't been a straight path. Balancing restaurant life and family life hasn't been easy. Along the way, we've faced enough challenges to fill a whole other book, and, like everyone else, endured a pandemic. There have also been bright spots, like the birth of our two beautiful children. But through it all, sitting down together at the table has kept us grounded. There's no better day off for us than one spent hanging out at home as a family and cooking together, like we did when we first met. It's different now, with the kids and more responsibilities, but the pleasure and joy of feeding each other still remain.

When we start the day, there's usually toasted Rakkenji shokupan (naturally fermented milk bread) on the table. Our Sunday brunch is a Japanese breakfast, with miso soup and rice, delicate tamagoyaki (dashi rolled omelet) and a host of vegetable dishes, such as gomaae broccoli (broccoli with sesame sauce) and spinach ohitashi (spinach with soy sauce and bonito flakes). Lunch might involve onigiri (rice balls) and Japanese sandos (sandwiches), both perfect for eating on the go. Dinner may take the form of a simple noodle dish like yakisoba, roasted kabocha squash smothered in mirin-sweetened ground pork, or a hotpot feast, a relaxed, interactive way to cook at the table. It's not all strictly Japanese. There are pizza nights and pho and lots and lots of pasta. The next day, we usually repurpose the leftovers into bento boxes for our kids' lunches.

We've seen Japanese food come a long way in this country—it's no longer viewed as just sushi and teriyaki. But many Americans still regard it as the domain of chefs and experts, and we seek to change that. These are dishes you can definitely make yourself, as most of them are simple enough to cook for your family or friends on a weeknight. Japanese home cooking is comforting, humble, and achievable by anyone. The purchase of just a few pantry items can easily make it part of your standard repertoire. We're not rigid about tradition, but the recipes are very much rooted in Japanese flavors, ingredients, and cooking techniques. Our book is a primer for home cooks who are eager to integrate Japanese flavors into their everyday meals. If you are already fluent in Japanese ingredients, we also use them in unexpected and delicious ways that may surprise you.

When we cook at the restaurant, we like to create something for people that they wouldn't make at home. At home, we're looking for the opposite—something that we can make over and over again, that is achievable, simple, and satisfying, and that we can potentially execute while holding an infant. As two working chefs, we used to have dinner around 9 or 9:30 p.m. Now we're on the clock, and get food on the table by 6 or 7. Our son is seven years old and eats most everything, while our two-year-old daughter is hopefully following in his footsteps. By a certain time, we have to give them baths and put them to bed, and dinner has to fit into a certain parameter. More often than not, it's about making rice, a protein, and then convincing our daughter to try a carrot. Our cooking has become a lot more practical, but it's still important that pleasure has a place at the table.

As much as we look to Japan for inspiration, the cooking in our home is also influenced by what's around us. Seasonal eating is central to both Japanese cuisine and ours. We pack up our kids and a week's worth of compost and go shopping every Saturday, choosing produce from the great vendors that come to our neighborhood farmers' market at McCarren Park in Brooklyn. Depending on where you are, you can find some of the best Japanese ingredients locally. Our favorite vegetables come from Bodhitree Farm, which grows an amazing array of Asian specialty produce.

Between spring and early winter, we get a majority of the vegetables we eat at home from them, whether it's shishito peppers, nasu (eggplant), daikon radishes, or satsumaimo (Japanese sweet potatoes). Hauling back a refrigerator's worth every week with two kids is a lot of work, but totally worth it.

In this book we wrestled, and wrestled some more, with the details of each recipe, recognizing that everyone's home kitchen is a little different. We've included many cues, through sight, smell, touch, or taste, to guide you through them. Of course, cooking is an imperfect science, and requires you to use your senses, experience, and knowledge of your own equipment. Not everyone has the same set of pots; no two ovens or burners function identically. And we know how subjective taste can be. What is too much salt for some, is not enough for others. So when you are trying out these recipes, keep in mind what you like and the equipment you're using, but most of all, trust your instincts. Nothing would make us happier than seeing you use our recipes as a jumping-off point—like Sawa did with her mother's so many years ago—and eventually making them your own.

From Hiroshima to Texas to New York

By Sawa

In 1995 I moved from Hiroshima to Denton, Texas, to go to college. Before then I hadn't realized how good I had it. And by that I mean, I didn't realize how good the food I grew up eating had been. It didn't dawn on me until I came to the US and had no Japanese food around me whatsoever.

American food came as a shock. I was eighteen years old and living in a dormitory for my first two years at the University of North Texas. I didn't have my own kitchen, so I ate in the cafeteria. I just wasn't used to it, so for the first two months I ate mostly from the salad bar. The pickings were slim—red and green Jell-O, croutons, cucumbers, dressings like Thousand Island and ranch. It was nothing like my high school cafeteria, where I could have gotten a bowl of udon or soba noodles, curry rice (fluffy steamed white rice with a thick curry-spiced gravy), katsu-don (a panko-fried pork cutlet simmered with dashi and eggs over rice), or a variety of sandwiches, like tamago (a creamy egg salad made with Kewpie mayonnaise).

Unlike most college students, I lost ten pounds when I went away to school. I craved food from home, but it was difficult to find in my tiny college town. Anyway, the idea of Japanese food in the States back then didn't go far beyond the California roll. The closest thing we had was Mr. Chopsticks, a restaurant that served a mash-up of Chinese and Thai. If I was going to eat the way I did at home, I'd have to learn how to make it myself. For me, that started with plain rice, miso soup, and noodles—the staples I needed to feel happy and nourished.

Today you can order pretty much anything you need online, but in the mid-1990s that was definitely not the case. I asked an older Japanese friend to take me to a supermarket where I could get some Japanese ingredients. I didn't have any cooking equipment either. In my third year, I finally moved into an apartment with a kitchen and I got a rice cooker. Then, I asked my mom to send me a Japanese cookbook, which I still have to this day. It had all the basics. Some of the first things I made were nikujaga, which means "meat and potato" in Japanese. It's pretty much potatoes, carrots, and beef braised in soy, mirin, and sake. I also made curry, because it's easy. And lots of fried rice. I followed the recipes precisely, and they came out pretty well. It was such a satisfying feeling, following a recipe and making the food that I wanted to eat. It made me feel like I was home.

When I wanted to make my mom's recipes, I would ask her for them over the phone and write down what she told me. I craved recipes for everyday things like okazu, which means anything you eat with rice. Dishes like kinpira, which is skinny matchsticks of burdock and carrots cooked down in sesame oil and chile, then braised in sake, mirin, and soy. Or hijiki, a type of seaweed that is prepared in a similar way, with soybeans, aburaage (fried tofu skin), carrots, fish cakes, or meat.

Of course she didn't have the measurements. When I pressed her, she would say, "I don't have a recipe!" She used the word *tekito* to describe the quantities, which means something like "suitable amount." Everything was "this much" of this and "that much" of that. So I had to remember what it tasted like and, through trial and error, I learned to re-create her cooking. Sometimes I would get very close to how she would do it and sometimes I decided to add to a recipe and make it my own. Looking back, this is how I got into cooking. I wasn't thinking about making it my profession. I just wanted to eat the way I was eating before.

When I was about to graduate from college, I attended a job fair for Japanese companies recruiting Japanese students in the US. I felt so out of place. Everyone was wearing the same thing—dark suits and ties—and you had to speak in a very formal and respectful way. I put on a suit to fit in and dyed my bleached blond hair, a college experiment, back to black. They asked questions like, "What do you think you can contribute to our company?" I realized that I didn't care, and that I didn't belong in that world. Cooking, on the other hand, was something I could see myself doing.

I moved to New York to go to culinary school. Many more Japanese ingredients were suddenly available to me, so it got much easier to make the food I love. Through my education and just gaining more experience, I became a better cook. But I didn't realize other people would love the food that I grew up with, too. One memory that stands out was during my time at Annisa, the Michelin-starred restaurant in the West Village where I worked under my chef and mentor, Anita Lo. When I was making staff meals every week, a lot of the time I was assigned a protein that I had to make work. Once I was a sous-chef and could order what I wanted, I started making hambagu, a Japanese meat patty. It's usually ground beef and pork with onion, carrots, and some bread crumbs soaked in milk, shaped into a patty, kind of like a meatloaf in hamburger form. (I like to add zucchini and tofu to mine.) You sear both sides, then make a pan sauce with a little bit of ketchup, Worcestershire, soy sauce, and honey that you pour on top. You eat it with rice. I'm so used to it that I didn't feel there was anything special about hambagu, but for the first time, I saw people eating my food and they were simply delighted by it.

The more I cooked for people, the more I understood that my food had appeal beyond my own nostalgia. This was definitely the case when I met my husband, Aaron, in 2011. He was and continues to be the most enthusiastic recipient of all the Japanese dishes I make, and of Japanese food in general. We are both chefs, so naturally, our love story took place over food. We were night people. We got off work late and rarely had evenings off. When we did, we would go out to eat, and when we didn't, we would cook. The times that we would usually hang out were between 11 p.m. and 1:30 p.m., which meant late-night meals and elaborate breakfasts. We bonded over off-the-menu dishes in Chinatown and nose-to-tail Korean barbecue feasts, impressing each other with how we ordered. On a date at one of our favorite ramen spots, Aaron, whose background is Eastern-European Jewish, wowed me with his deep appreciation of Japanese cooking by ordering takowasa, raw octopus mixed with wasabi stems. It was then I knew that I could take him to Japan, which I eventually did.

The first home-cooked Japanese meal I made for Aaron was in the tiny kitchen of my first real one-bedroom apartment, in a fourth-floor walk-up in Crown Heights, Brooklyn. I had to sit on a small stool just to be able to reach into the back of the mini-fridge. Aaron said it was like Narnia, a portal into my world. It was a hot day. I opened a package of Sanuki udon noodles from a special stash my mother had mailed to me. These thick, chewy noodles are from Kagawa prefecture, which is where my grandmother is from. It's the noodle I grew up with and the noodle I crave. I thought, this is a special noodle that I want to share with my new boyfriend. I served him chilled Sanuki udon on a bamboo mat, with a dashi-soy dipping sauce and sautéed pork with eggplant. We sat at my table and drank shochu. Aaron loved it, and it's become one of his favorite meals.

Many more home-cooked meals followed. I cooked Aaron a favorite from my hometown, Hiroshima-style okonomiyaki with pork belly. One morning, I made us a simple breakfast of rice, miso soup, and natto—the pungent fermented soybeans—mixed with karashi mustard and dashi soy, and he was crazy about it. I was thinking, "He really loves Japanese food," because you can't fake liking natto. He later cooked some delicious natto fried rice with a few packs I'd given him because he wanted his dad to try it. Once, he made sushi to surprise me, and I gave him some advice on how to roll it better. I think I said, "You're bold for making me sushi. I used to work at a sushi restaurant!" Aaron laughed and said, "I'm pretty good, aren't I?" That scored him some points. By then I realized that the person I wanted to be with had to like the food I love, and he was just that.

Homemade Sushi on Long Island

By Aaron

In our house, Sawa is the expert on Japanese food. I've come to love and appreciate it almost as much as she does, though I came to it in a much more indirect way. Growing up in a predominantly Jewish town on Long Island, I had the understanding of Japanese food that you might expect of a typical American kid in the '80s and '90s, limited mostly to teriyaki and the sushi buffet at bar mitzvahs. I enjoyed California rolls, but I was squeamish about raw fish. That all changed one night in high school when my parents brought home sushi from a local restaurant. I had requested a California roll and a smoked salmon roll, both of which I really enjoyed. When I later found out from my parents that I had unwittingly eaten raw salmon (an honest mistake on their part), I was like oh, this is good! Then the floodgates opened.

Once I discovered my love of sushi, I started to ask my parents to order it way too frequently. At a certain point they told me, "We can't order sushi all the time, it's expensive!" My mom and I got a VHS video from the library on how to make sushi—it was the early nineties, so there was no YouTube—and I got some basic sushi-making books, materials, and ingredients. If I was going to cook Japanese food, I needed to have really good fish. I found a store two towns over called Shin Nippon Do. They had Japanese cucumbers, avocado, nori sheets, and rice vinegar, and a refrigerated section with tuna, fluke, and frozen raw shrimp, and those fake crab sticks for my beloved California rolls. Then I would spend the day preparing sushi at home. I'd cook a pot of rice, use another pot to make the sushi zu (sweet-salty vinegar seasoning for the rice), fry some shrimp tempura—you can imagine what our kitchen looked like after this. It took hours to make what would be devoured in minutes. My friends loved the free sushi. My family enjoyed my efforts, too, even if as a young, very novice cook, I created a bit more of a mess than anyone wanted.

To be fair, I had always been a good eater, and I took an interest in cooking early on. It started as a practical way to help around the house. My mother was having health troubles, and she would get tired at the end of the day, so my brother and I needed to chip in. I wasn't really a laundry person (I'm still not), but cooking was something that was productive and useful, and I enjoyed doing it. I eventually realized that if I learned how to cook something, I could eat it whenever I wanted.

Like Sawa, I ended up cooking for myself in college. I went to the Maryland Institute College of Art to study my other passion, painting. Each dorm room had a kitchen, and because it was a small school, the meal options were limited. By the time second semester rolled around, I went off the college meal plan and ended up cooking for myself and my roommate. It was a barter system—he had the car so he could drive me to the market, and I cooked for him in return. By the time I was a sophomore, I knew I wanted to go to culinary school. My parents encouraged me to finish my education. But as soon as I graduated, I moved back to New York and immediately got a job as a line cook.

When I met Sawa on a setup years later, I had been cooking at Italian restaurants for a while and was ready to move in a different direction. I was interested in Jewish food, and exploring my culinary roots. Early on in our relationship, I made matzoh ball soup for Sawa. Mine was a complex version, where I cooked the broth from the bones, poached the breast, ground the thighs and mixed them with chicken liver to make kreplach (a type of dumpling), and rendered the fat for the matzoh balls. At the time, I was still looking for the right noodle. I tried Manischewitz egg noodles and fresh lo mein, which is what I put in the soup the night I made it for her. She said, "You should use ramen noodles in this." To her it was so obvious, but I don't know how long it would have taken me to figure it out. Once we hit the ramen button on the matzoh ball soup, we never went back. In retrospect, that was the beginning of the cuisine we would create together at our restaurant, and a preview of how we would cook in our home.

Contributor's Note

By Gabriella Gershenson

Being a first-generation American, like Sawa's and Aaron's kids, I have a special kinship with this project, and an appreciation for the not-insignificant task of instilling culture through food in a country that's not your own. I also understand firsthand the pressure to assimilate. The US is a melting pot, not a mosaic. In this context, I have been in awe of Sawa's ability to deepen her relationship to her culture while living outside of it. Having Japanese-speaking children and cooking mostly Japanese food at home despite not having lived there for nearly thirty years is impressive. It's also a testament to Aaron, who has adopted Sawa's customs, and, in lockstep with her, is passing them on to their kids. Having witnessed their young son, Kaishu, devouring ikura (salmon roe) by the spoonful, and Mayako, their daughter, cramming her mouth with gooey natto by the age of one, it was clear Sawa and Aaron must be doing something right.

The first time I came to their home in Brooklyn for a meal several years ago, we were just starting work on the book together. Ostensibly, I was there to watch them cook, and help deepen my understanding of what they do. But I was also just excited at the prospect of digging into a home-cooked Japanese meal.

The dinner was casual to them, but it made a lasting impression on me. When I arrived, Sawa was leaning over a steaming pot, stirring udon noodles with a pair of cooking chopsticks. Aaron was setting the table on their terrace, which was home to mismatched pots, climbing vines, and shiso plants. Most items on the table were familiar, while others were completely novel, such as a plastic hand-crank sesame mill that, like many Japanese objects, was extremely specific and inexplicably endearing.

Sawa arranged the noodles in a shallow platter and topped them with ice cubes, something I had never seen done before. She told me that, in Japan, this is how they keep the noodles cold while enjoying them. Once she explained it, I thought, right, of course! It was at once obvious, and brilliant. This was the first of many moments like these, when she would explain the logic of Japanese food, and I would be struck by its perfect simplicity.

When it was time to eat, Sawa and Aaron showed me how to set myself up, with a bowl of smoky dashi-tsuyu dipping sauce that I could doctor with the garnishes on the table any way I liked—lemon zest, scallions, shredded nori, and of course freshly ground sesame seeds. We dunked the noodles into our bowls to soak up the flavors of the sauce. As my bowl ran low, I replenished it with more of everything, supplementing with seasonings as I went, making each bite its own.

When I left, I was struck by how special the meal was, unlike any I had ever had, but also spare, even humble. A few weeks later, I asked Sawa for the recipe, and bought the ingredients I needed from Sunrise Mart on Broome Street. At home in my apartment, I mixed up the dipping sauce, boiled water for the noodles, and made sure that my ice trays were full. Modeling my meal after Sawa's and Aaron's, I assembled small bowls of garnishes, pulled out a platter for the iced udon, poured the sauce into a bowl and sat down to eat, marveling at how I could reproduce something I hadn't known weeks before, and that it still held the power to delight. I have felt that way since then about so many of their recipes in this book. As you cook from it, I hope you have similar revelations, and moments of discovery and joy. I would want nothing more than to pass that feeling on to you.

Pantry and Kitchen Staples

Most of our recipes call for ingredients that you already have at home or can easily find at the supermarket, plus a few key Japanese pantry staples. If you don't have them, it won't take much to stock up on the basics. In this chapter we share the Japanese ingredients that appear in many of our recipes and are on regular rotation in our kitchen. Most of them are shelf-stable or will keep in the fridge or freezer for a long time, so they'll be there when you need them.

Bonito Flakes Bonito flakes, known in Japanese as katsuobushi, are whisper-thin shavings of dried, smoked bonito, a fish that's a member of the tuna family. It takes months of aging to cure it; when it's ready, the flesh is hard as wood and is then shaved into flakes. These usually come in a bag and look like wood chips. They are shelf-stable and should keep for months. Store them in an airtight container or in a resealable plastic bag in your pantry. If your kitchen is humid, stash them in the freezer or refrigerator to protect them from moisture. We like Kaneso brand from Hiroshima, which is available online and at Japanese or Asian groceries.

Dashi Powder Just add water to get a quick and easy instant version of dashi broth. Powdered dashi comes in a variety of flavors like the standard bonito and kombu,

niboshi (dried sardine), dried shiitake, and ago (flying fish). We seek out brands that are free of additives and preservatives, such as Kayanoya USA, which ships to your door.

Kewpie Mayonnaise Kewpie is our favorite mayonnaise and is what you'll find in most Japanese homes. Compared to American mayo, it's richer, creamier, and tangier. It's made using egg yolks only. There's no sugar, and the other main ingredients are rice vinegar and vegetable oil.

Konnyaku (see Konnyaku, page 20)

Kuro Neri Goma (Black Sesame Paste) This is a rich, nutty paste made from roasted black sesame seeds that's often used in desserts, but is great in savory recipes, too. The color is inky and dramatic. Since it's rich in oil, refrigerate to keep fresh, and stir before using if it separates.

Mirin A naturally sweet Japanese rice wine used exclusively in cooking, mirin is like the Art Garfunkel of ingredients—sweet-voiced, always the counterpoint, never the star. Like Art, it's essential for balancing other foods. It's often used in conjunction with salty and savory ingredients, such as soy sauce, sake, and dashi, to create foundational Japanese flavors. We prefer using hon-mirin, a 14% alcohol wine made with rice and rice koji, which you can purchase online or in a well-stocked Japanese grocery store. If you can only find the more common aji-mirin, a mirin-like ingredient that often contains additives like corn syrup and

glucose, that still works. Store hon-mirin in your pantry, but refrigerate aji-mirin after opening.

Miso (see Miso and Shio Koji, page 23)

Noodles

Malony (aka glass noodles) are straight, thin, gluten-free noodles made from potato starch. They have a springy texture that's great at absorbing flavor. They are sold alongside other dried noodles in Asian grocery stores.

Ramen are wheat-flour, machine-made noodles that range in thickness and texture, and can be curly or straight. They contain kansui (sodium bicarbonate), which

gives them their characteristic springiness. Ramen noodles are available fresh or dried, but try to get them fresh or from the freezer if you can. We use **temomi**, a thick, wavy noodle, as well as a thinner, more classic variety from Sun Noodle, a company that makes fresh ramen that is consistently excellent.

Soba, which means "buckwheat" in Japanese, is a buckwheat noodle. Since buckwheat is gluten-free, soba noodles are often made with wheat flour to introduce elasticity to the dough. In the US, soba is most commonly sold dried.

Somen, a thin wheat noodle made with flour, water, and salt, must be 1.3 millimeters thick or less to be called somen. In Japan, somen is

KONNYAKU

Konnyaku is the Japanese word for a plant called konjac, a distant cousin of the taro root. Raw konjac is hardly edible, but once it's peeled and pulverized, processed with water and calcium hydroxide, and boiled, it becomes the chewy, bouncy food called konnyaku. In Japan, konnyaku has been eaten for centuries. It's low in calories and high in fiber, which makes it popular with dieters. It has no flavor, but is excellent at soaking up the seasonings it's cooked with and comes in all different shapes and sizes.

Common varieties include **ita konnyaku ❶**, which is brick-shaped and tinted gray from the addition of seaweed. **Shirataki ❷**, also called **ito konnyaku ❸**, looks like a noodle. (*Shirataki* literally means "white waterfall," and the name comes from the way konnyaku puree looks when it's pushed through a ricer.) **Tama konnyaku ❹** is small and ball shaped, and can be added to braises or stews. You can find most konnyaku in the refrigerated section of an Asian grocery store, and shirataki at many American markets, too.

considered a summertime food. The wispy noodles are usually served cold with a dipping sauce.

Udon is a type of noodle made from wheat flour, water, and salt. The dough is kneaded extensively to develop the gluten, which gives udon their characteristic chewiness. In Japan, there are various styles and thicknesses. Some of our favorites are **Inaniwa** from Akita prefecture, which are silky, thin, and usually sold dried. Another is **Sanuki** from Kagawa prefecture, which are thick and chewy, and are usually sold dried or semi-dried. The latter can be stored at room temperature, but they don't keep as long as fully dried noodles. **Sanuki-style udon**, which is very similar in shape to Sanuki udon, is not made to the same exacting standards. You can find these parcooked in the freezer section of the Asian grocer.

Okonomi Sauce This sweet, savory, tangy condiment belongs on top of okonomiyaki (see Hiroshima-Style Okonomiyaki, page 81), but is also great with Tonkatsu (page 193) and sandwiches (pages 106–116). You can buy it—our favorite brand is Otafuku from Hiroshima—or easily make your own (see Okonomi Sauce, page 34).

Panko This is a type of dried bread crumb—the word means "bread powder." It's used in the same way as regular bread crumbs, but panko crumbs are larger, resulting in flakier, crunchier food when fried.

Ponzu An essential Japanese dipping sauce, ponzu is a mixture of soy, mirin, and citrus. Its acidity makes it a natural match for rich foods. You can buy commercially made ponzu at any Asian grocer; our favorite is Umaji Mura Yuzu Ponzu. Or in a few minutes, you can make your own (see Ponzu, page 36).

Rice

Japanese white rice is a short-grain, polished rice that's essential to Japanese cooking. When rice is "polished," that means the hull, bran, and germ are removed. This makes the grain whiter, quicker-cooking, starchy, and easier to digest. Unlike some long-grain varieties that remain separate when cooked, short-grain rice sticks together, which is why it's perfect for making Onigiri (page 218) and Temaki Zushi (page 168).

In the US, Japanese-grown rice can be expensive and hard to find. Our favorite source is The Rice Factory (see Sources, page 252), which imports many varieties, including each year's new crop. California-grown short-grain white rice is a good substitute. A common brand found in American supermarkets is Nishiki, but we prefer Matsuri, Kagayaki, and Tamaki Gold. Store at room temperature in an airtight container to keep fresh and protected from unwanted visitors.

Japanese brown rice also comes in several varieties. We use haiga-mai, a name that refers to the part of the rice that's left behind after polishing. It has the nutrients of brown rice, but cooks quickly, like white rice. Store it the way you would white rice.

Japanese multigrain rice is a nutritious rice blend that includes brown, red, and black rice, rye berries, and two kinds of barley. You can buy this at a Japanese or Asian grocer; we like the Kagayaki brand.

Rice Vinegar Japanese rice vinegar, made from fermented glutinous rice and/or fermented sake lees, is a go-to in our kitchen. Compared to sharper vinegars like red or white wine vinegar, this one is fairly neutral, with a well-rounded flavor. Rice vinegar and vinegar labeled "rice wine vinegar" are one and the same, something to keep in mind when shopping. We like Mizkan and Iio Jozo Fujisu brands.

Sake A Japanese rice wine that we use frequently in our cooking, it's more mellow and less acidic than white wine, and has a softer flavor and a touch of sweetness. When buying sake for cooking, buy an inexpensive bottle that's decent enough to drink, but not too good, keeping in mind that when you heat it, it will lose the more nuanced flavors. Be sure to buy the sake from a liquor or wine store, because the sake sold in grocery stores in most states will be "cooking sake," which has added salt.

Salt (Shio) We mainly use two types of salt at home: kosher salt, which is coarse like sand, and Japanese sea salt, which is fine, a bit moist, and higher in salinity. We like the Setouchi No Moshio brand of Japanese salt—moshio means "seaweed salt," and Setouchi is the region that surrounds the Seto Inland Sea. Our kosher salt of choice is Diamond Crystal. Others, such as Morton's, can have a higher salinity level and result in a saltier outcome. So stick with Diamond in the recipes that call for kosher salt, or adjust the quantity as needed if you are using a different brand.

Seaweed

Aonori is a green seaweed that's usually ground into a powder and used as a seasoning. It's particularly good on deep-fried food—the taste of the seaweed blooms from the heat, releasing a salty, umami flavor. Aonori should be used soon after opening, otherwise the bright green color oxidizes and the flavor dissipates.

Hijiki is a type of seaweed that is widely available in Japan. It's almost always sold dried, and must be rehydrated before use. Hijiki ranges in color from dark brown to black, and has a mild sea flavor.

Kombu is Japanese for dried kelp. Combined with bonito flakes it makes dashi, the Japanese mother stock. Just a small piece of kombu gives food an intangible savoriness (aka umami). When you're shopping for kombu, the price usually indicates the quality. The more expensive it is, the higher the grade. A lower-grade kombu is a good choice for recipes like braises and miso soup, which include other flavoring components, while

TOFU

The process of making tofu is a bit like making cheese—instead of cow's milk coagulated with rennet, tofu is soy milk coagulated with nigari, which is magnesium chloride derived from seawater. Tofu is nutritious and high in protein, and because of its uniquely adaptable texture and neutral flavor, you can use it in so many ways.

Silken tofu ❶ is the lightest and creamiest of tofu textures. Soft tofu is similar, but with a slightly grainier consistency, while **medium-firm tofu** ❷ is still jiggly but holds its shape better. We avoid firm tofu, which tends to be dry and spongy. Choose tofu depending on what you're making. For instance, don't use silken tofu in a stir-fry, or it will fall apart in the pan. We like to buy organic tofu, which is also non-GMO, and store leftovers in fresh water in the fridge. The more frequently you change the water the longer it will keep—usually up to a week.

There is also fried tofu, which can be bought fresh or frozen at Asian and some American grocery stores. **Aburaage** ❸—from the word for "oil-fried"—is tofu that has been thinly sliced and then fried twice, producing a thin packet that can be opened up and stuffed. Its spongy texture sucks up the flavor of anything it is cooked in, like braises or soups. **Atsuage tofu** ❹ is a block of fried tofu with a lovely golden exterior. The frying pulls out a good deal of moisture, so it holds its shape well when cut and is particularly good for simmering or stir-fries.

high-grade kombu is better suited for dashi, or other dishes where the flavor of the kombu is the focus. Seal your kombu well. Stored correctly, it can last for years.

Nori is like edible paper—it's made from red algae that's harvested, shredded, dried, and formed into sheets. Americans know nori best as a sushi wrapper, but in Japan, it's a widely used ingredient. Nori adds visual drama to a dish and has a unique texture that starts out crackly, then softens into something chewy, with a distinct ocean flavor. You can buy it in all different shapes and sizes, from large sheets to confetti-like slivers, known as **kizami-nori**. **Ajitsuke-nori** has been brushed with a seasoning and are smaller sheets. These are typically used as a snack for kids, or to wrap Onigiri (page 218).

We look for nori that are made in Japan, with a nice sheen and a dark, deep green color. Store in a tightly sealed plastic bag with the "demoisturizer" pack it comes with to retain the texture. If it gets soft, toast the individual sheets by carefully waving them over an open flame for a few seconds per side to dry out, but be careful since it can burn quickly.

Wakame is dark green in color with a slightly briny flavor. It's sold both fresh and dried, but the latter version is more widely available. Dried wakame doesn't need to be washed—just throw it into soup to rehydrate, or if using in salad, soak it in water for a few minutes, then blot it dry in paper towels before dressing.

———

MISO AND SHIO KOJI

Koji (*Aspergillus oryzae*) is the catalyzing mold for fermentation in many umami-rich Japanese staples. It's a main ingredient in fermented pastes such as miso and shio koji, made from soybeans and rice respectively, that are mixed with salt and koji and left for months in a cool, dark place to develop a salty, umami flavor.

Miso, which is made from cooked, mashed soybeans, comes in infinite varieties, ranging from sweet and pale (like **saikyo shiro miso** ❶) to dark and robust (such as **aka miso** ❷). The younger the miso is, the lighter and milder it tends to be, as it gets darker and more intensely flavored with age. Since there are so many kinds, we recommend trying a few to get a sense of what you like. We like to go natural and organic. If you're only going to buy one, we recommend the versatile **awase miso** ❸ (blended miso), which isn't super strong or dark, nor is it as sweet as a light miso.

Shio koji ❹ is made from salt, water, and rice that's been inoculated with koji. It's an umami magnifier, coaxing depths of flavor out of whatever it's paired with. Like miso, shio koji is meant to enhance the flavor of a dish, and not be eaten alone.

You can find both miso and shio koji in the refrigerated aisle of a Japanese grocer; miso is also available at most well-stocked supermarkets and health food stores.

Sesame Seeds Whether whole, ground, or pureed into a smooth paste, sesame seeds are widely used in both sweet and savory preparations. To get the best flavor out of sesame seeds, we buy them toasted and often re-toast them in a pan over medium heat, stirring often, until they become aromatic. The vitamins and minerals in sesame seeds are best absorbed if they've been crushed, so pulverize them in a sesame grinder or with a mortar and pestle (see Suribachi, page 30) before adding to food.

Shichimi Togarashi A classic Japanese spice mix that, as the word *shichi* (which means "seven") suggests, is made up of seven ingredients: togarashi (chile powder), sansho pepper, orange zest, black and white sesame seeds, white poppy seeds, and aonori. In Japan, you can go to a shop that will custom blend the ratios to your liking. These days, you can find it in the spice aisle of American grocery stores.

Shio Koji (see Miso and Shio Koji, page 23)

Soy Sauce This salty liquid, fermented from soybeans and often wheat, is the seasoning most associated with Japanese food. The most common type of soy sauce (called shoyu in Japanese) is **koikuchi**, which is dark and has a salty, umami-rich flavor. **Tamari** is a gluten-free alternative fermented from soy only. You can substitute tamari for soy sauce in any of our recipes. All soy sauces should be refrigerated.

Tofu (see Tofu, page 22)

Tsukemono These Japanese pickles, a staple of every meal that are usually eaten with rice, are cured in some combination of salt, sugar, and/or vinegar. Every city has its own type specific to its region, and every season has its own pickle. Some of the more common ones you'll find in Japanese stores in the US are takuan (yellow daikon), umeboshi plums, and tiny green cucumber slices called kyurizuke.

Yuzu Juice Yuzu is a Japanese citrus fruit that is floral and fresh, sweeter than a lemon or a lime and more complex. Since fresh yuzu can be hard to find, bottled yuzu juice is the next best thing. (A substitute would be fresh Meyer lemon juice, or 4 parts fresh lemon juice to 1 part fresh grapefruit juice.) Before using the bottled juice, give it a shake, and refrigerate after opening.

Yuzu Kosho This unique fermented condiment is made from salt, chiles, and yuzu juice and zest. There are two varieties: a milder, more citrus-forward green one made with unripened yuzu and green chiles, and a spicier red version made from ripe yellow yuzu and red chiles. Keep the jar refrigerated, and try to use it within a year, before the flavors start to fade.

Japanese Produce

We love eating Japanese produce, which can be found at Japanese or Asian grocers or at specialty stands at farmers' markets. It's also available online at Suzuki Farm, a farm in Delmar, Delaware, that ships vegetables grown exclusively from Japanese seeds. We try to support local agriculture and buy vegetables that are responsibly grown, organically or without chemicals.

Daikon Radish ❶ These radishes aren't too spicy and are sometimes sweet. They are great eaten raw (crunchy) and braised (silky and meaty). The tops are nutritious and excellent braised or pickled. Look for a heavy one with fresh tops. Since daikon ranges in size greatly—from about 8 inches to a few feet—it's hard to say what is a "small" radish versus a "large" one. For that reason, we provide the weight for them in our recipes.

Gobo (Burdock) ❷ This earthy root vegetable grows up to three feet long and is high in fiber. Scrub clean using a tawashi brush (see page 30), but don't take off all the brown skin. That's where much of the flavor is.

Kabocha ❸ This autumn squash has a firm, deep-orange flesh that's starchier than other varieties, but still very sweet. They're great for roasting, braising, and steaming.

Kabu (Turnip) ❹ These turnips have sweet, silky flesh and are delicious cooked, or eaten raw when they're small (the little ones are often sold as Hakurei turnips). Kabu can range in size from tiny when harvested young to quite large if they are left to grow. The tops are good for braising.

Mitsuba ❺ This herb looks a bit like parsley with fewer leaves, and it tastes similar, with a hint of celery thrown in. It's especially good in soups.

Nagaimo (Mountain Yam) ❻ Also known as yamaimo, or Japanese mountain potato, this is one of few tubers that is eaten both raw and cooked. It has a special gluey texture that in Japanese is called neba-neba, similar to okra or natto. Nagaimo are often sold packed in sawdust, which helps keep them dry. They can be stored in a cool dry place for months.

Napa Cabbage 7 More delicate than green or savoy cabbage and milder in flavor, napa cabbage cooks quickly, and has a crunchy texture when eaten raw. It can keep for weeks in the refrigerator.

Nasu (Japanese Eggplant) 8 These skinny eggplants are smaller than European varieties, deep purple, have no bitterness, and range in size from six inches to about a foot. You can substitute the Chinese variety, which are also long and narrow, and a lighter shade of purple.

Satoimo (Taro) 9 This small variety of Japanese taro potato has hairy, coconut-like skin and flesh that is creamy and silky once cooked. It is technically a root, not a potato, but the suffix "imo" means "potato" in Japanese and covers a broader range of tubers and root vegetables. Store in a brown paper bag or wrapped in newspaper in a cool, dry place.

Satsumaimo (Japanese Sweet Potato) 10 Sweet but starchier than American sweet potatoes, satsumaimo have purplish skin and white flesh that turns yellow when it's roasted. The longer you roast them, the sweeter they get. Store in a cool, dark place and they'll keep through the winter.

Scallions 11 These probably appear in more of our recipes than any other vegetable. Eat them thinly sliced and raw as a garnish, or cut into larger pieces and cooked. Both the white and green parts are delicious.

Shishito 12 These small peppers are about the size of a thumb. Look for a deep green color, but don't be afraid of the occasional red one. The color doesn't affect your one in ten chances of getting a spicy one.

Shiso 13 This type of perilla plant also goes by the name ōba, and is floral and distinctly Japanese. It grows in green and purple varieties—green tends to be more fragrant. You can buy it year-round at Asian markets, but it's easy to grow, and abundant in our garden in the summertime.

Shungiku (Chrysanthemum Greens) 14 This leafy green has a wonderful, aromatic grassy flavor, cooks quickly, and is especially good sautéed or prepared in a hotpot.

Spinach 15 We like to buy spinach in bunches, which is how it is sold in Japan, with big leaves and hardy, pinkish stems. Wash at least three times to remove the sand and grit. Spinach is also very similar in appearance and flavor to komatsuna, another leafy green vegetable that is common in Japanese cooking.

Tokyo Negi 16 This very large scallion looks like a leek but has more tender flesh. It gives great oniony flavor and is excellent braised.

Yuzu 17 This citrus looks like a lemon but has a floral aroma and flavor that is synonymous with Japanese food. Getting a fresh yuzu is a real treat. We like to use it all by grating the zest into soups and squeezing the juice. We even throw the spent pith in the bath to give it a nice yuzu aroma.

Kyoto Ninjin (Kyoto Carrot) 18 This carrot has a deep orange, almost red flesh. The Japanese like to use them in osechi, Japanese New Year's food, for their vibrant color.

Mushrooms

Maitake (Hen of the Woods) 19 These woodsy mushrooms must be cooked and are wonderful for roasting and braising. Store in a paper bag in the refrigerator. Mushrooms don't like being wrapped in plastic—they'll sweat and go bad quickly.

Shiitake 20 Shiitake have a hearty, sweet, woodsy flavor and a silky, meaty texture when cooked. Look for mushrooms with nice brown caps with white undersides.

Shimeji (White Beech Mushrooms) 21 These mild-flavored mushrooms have an appealing silky-but-firm texture. We like to pull them apart into little clusters before we cook them.

Equipment

These are the tools in our kitchen that we get the most use out of, and the majority of them are Japanese. Though we highly recommend cooking with them, they are not required to make the recipes in this book.

Butane Burner ❶ This portable burner allows you to cook on the tabletop. We use it for dishes like hotpot and sukiyaki, and even take it to our balcony for grilling. You need to buy butane gas canisters and replace them once they're empty. We like the Iwatani brand.

Cooking Chopsticks ❷ These extra-long chopsticks let you stir, whisk, flip, and pick up food. We can't cook without them.

Digital Scale Scales are important for measuring ingredients, because weight doesn't lie. For the baking recipes in our book, we strongly recommend using a scale for best results, which is why we list the weight measurements first.

Donabe Pot ❸ We use this earthenware or clay pot for simmering dishes such as hotpot. The thick ceramic retains heat well, and once it gets hot, it can keep the food inside warm for a while (it must have liquid in it when it gets hot, otherwise it can crack).

Japanese Knives Japan has many kinds of knives, each with a specialized purpose. It's hard to list them all here, but these are the ones we use most: Santoku ❹ and gyutu are both good multipurpose, everyday knives. Nakiri ❺ is a rectangular-shaped knife designed for cutting vegetables. There are also knives for butchering fish: deba, which are short, thick, and sturdy, and yanagi, which have long and thin blades, for cutting sashimi. We also always have a good serrated knife ❻ for cutting bread and tomatoes. Our favorite brands are Masamoto, Aritsugu, Takamura, and Nagomi. We like to sharpen our own knives. A small investment in a sharpening stone and some tutorials on the Internet can help you maintain them properly.

Oroshigane (Japanese Grater) ❼ *Oroshi* means "grating" and *gane* means "metal." Unlike American graters, these don't have holes. Instead, small spikes grate the food. Oroshigane are ideal for pulverizing daikon, ginger, or wasabi.

Otama (Ladles) ❽ There are many types of Japanese ladles for different purposes. For serving hotpot, you can use smaller ladles for the broth and slotted or perforated ladles for scooping up food when you don't want any liquid. These are indispensable for family-style meals.

Rice Cooker ❾ An electric rice cooker makes it easy to cook perfect rice at the push of a button, without using a burner and a pot. We like the Japanese brand Zojirushi.

Sesame Grinder ❿ Grinding sesame seeds releases their aroma and flavor. These grinders range from manual, hand-crank to electric ones that dispense ground sesame mechanically and have settings like fine, medium, and coarse.

Shamoji (Rice Paddle) ⓫ Use this to scoop rice and to mix sushi zu (vinegar mixed with salt, sugar, and kombu) into freshly cooked rice for sumeshi (sushi rice).

Suribachi and Surikogi (Mortar and Pestle) ⓬ A Japanese mortar, or suribachi, is a textured bowl usually made of unglazed ceramic. Surikogi is a Japanese pestle made of wood for grinding food in the suribachi. Small sets are good for grinding sesame seeds and spices, while larger ones are suitable for items like fish and mountain potatoes.

Tamagoyaki Pan ⓭ We use this rectangular pan every morning to make tamagoyaki for our kids' bentos. Also called a tamagoyaki-ki in Japanese, they come in different sizes and materials: Teflon-coated, copper, iron, and ceramic are all popular. A 5 × 7-inch pan is a good size for a 2- to 3-egg tamagoyaki.

Tawashi Brush ⓮ This durable Japanese brush with sturdy bristles made of hemp palm is great for cleaning root vegetables (especially if you plan to eat them with the skin on). We like the Kamenoko brand.

Yakiami Grill ⓯ This stainless steel rack with a handle is used to cook food over fire, or over an open flame on the stovetop. Since it has a slotted bottom, it's best for grilling anything that won't drip onto the stove. We use it for things like mochi, corn, and shishito peppers.

Yukihira Pots ⓰ These multipurpose pots with pouring spouts are ubiquitous in Japanese households. The most widely used ones are made of aluminum and pounded into shape, giving it its signature dimpled look. The handle is wood and replaceable when it gets old and loose.

TANZAKU CUT

Most of the cuts in this book are fairly standard, but one that is unique to Japan, with no Western equivalent, is the tanzaku cut. A tanzaku cut is a rectangular shape, usually reserved for daikon and carrots. The thickness varies depending on the dish—thinner for Tonjiru (page 197), thicker for hotpot (page 143). The name tanzaku comes from the shape of a special type of paper that you write poetry on, especially haikus. The pieces of food cut this way are easy to pick up with chopsticks and fit in your mouth in a single bite.

Step 1: Cut crosswise into 1½- to 2-inch-thick pieces.

Step 2: Place the cut-side down and slice into slabs ½ to ¾ inch thick.

Step 3: Stack the slabs and cut into strips ⅛ to ¼ inch wide.

Basics
基本のレシピ

These are quick recipes that represent an assortment of building blocks, condiments, and other essentials that we use in many of our recipes, or like to keep on hand in the fridge. Although some, like ponzu and okonomi sauce, can be store-bought, it's easy and worth it to make your own.

This is our recipe for traditional dashi, a foundational ingredient in Japanese cooking. It's the basic stock most Americans will know from miso and clear soups, but it's also used in stews and hotpots such as oden, for poaching rolled cabbage, in broth or dipping sauce for noodles, and mixed into okonomiyaki batter. We make our dashi with kombu (dried kelp) and bonito flakes. Kombu has a slightly salty, ocean-y taste that blends harmoniously with the bonito flakes, giving an excellent smoky umami flavor to the food.

MAKES 4 CUPS • TOTAL TIME: 55 MINUTES

Dashi

だし

4¼ cups cold water
1 piece of dried kombu
(roughly 4 × 4 inches)
1 cup lightly packed
bonito flakes

In a pot, combine the water and kombu and let sit for 30 minutes or up to overnight, to extract as much umami as you can. Warm over medium heat. When small bubbles start to come up from the bottom of the pot, just before it starts to boil, reduce the heat to low. Gently simmer until the kombu rehydrates and softens, about 10 minutes. Remove the kombu (discard or reserve for another use; see Notes).

Add the bonito flakes. Increase the heat to medium-high, bring to a boil, then reduce to a simmer and cook for 1 to 2 minutes, skimming any foam and impurities that come up to the surface. Remove from the heat. Strain through a fine-mesh sieve into a large bowl, gently squeezing the dashi out of the bonito flakes. If you don't have a fine-mesh sieve, you can use a colander lined with a paper towel. Use immediately or let cool to room temperature before storing in the refrigerator.

Refrigerate dashi for up to 4 days, or freeze for up to 3 months.

Notes After you retrieve the spent kombu from the finished broth, we recommend saving it to make Sweet Kombu (page 35). You can wrap it tightly and refrigerate it for up to 4 days before using.
    If you don't have the time to make dashi from scratch, for every 1 cup of dashi your recipe calls for, stir 1 teaspoon of dashi powder into 1 cup cold water.

Okonomi Sauce

Japanese Barbecue Sauce

お好みソース

½ cup ketchup
¼ cup Worcestershire sauce
1½ tablespoons soy sauce
1 tablespoon honey

This homemade sauce is so easy to make, and chances are you already have all of the ingredients at home. It's great drizzled on okonomiyaki (see Hiroshima-Style Okonomiyaki, page 81), but that sells it short. It's a fantastic all-purpose barbecue sauce—brushed on anything from grilled chicken to ribs to steak. If you're making the sauce for a single recipe, you'll probably have some left over. The good news is, it keeps for ages in the fridge.

MAKES ABOUT 1 CUP • TOTAL TIME: 5 MINUTES

In a small bowl, mix together the ketchup, Worcestershire, soy sauce, and honey until thoroughly combined. Store in an airtight container in the refrigerator for up to 1 year.

Chile Mayo

チリマヨ

½ cup Kewpie mayonnaise
1 teaspoon sriracha
¼ teaspoon rice vinegar

This addictive sauce is our version of the spicy mayonnaise you get at a sushi restaurant. We serve it with our Lox Bowl (page 167) but encourage you to try it anywhere you would normally use mayonnaise. It's great on a sando!

MAKES ½ CUP • TOTAL TIME: 3 MINUTES

In a small bowl, stir together the mayonnaise, sriracha, and vinegar until combined. Store in an airtight container in the refrigerator for up to 2 months.

I need to thank chef Anita Lo for this recipe. It's a great way to reuse the kombu leftover from making Dashi (page 33), which on its own is full of umami, but not much flavor. By braising the spent kombu in soy, mirin, and sugar, you transform it into a sweet-salty preserve. We use sweet kombu as a secret weapon in our Lox Bowl (page 167), but it's great over plain rice, too. We save the liquid that it's cooked in and have dubbed it "awesome sauce," because it's sweet, salty, and loaded with umami. We use it as a teriyaki-style glaze for Tsukune (page 187) and brush it over grilled Onigiri (page 218) for extra salty-sweet flavor. **—Sawa**

**MAKES ½ CUP SWEET KOMBU AND 1 CUP KOMBU "AWESOME SAUCE" •
TOTAL TIME: 10 MINUTES, OR 8 HOURS 10 MINUTES IF SOAKING THE KOMBU**

Cut the kombu into strips about ⅛ inch wide and 2 inches long.

In a small pot, combine the strips of kombu, the soy sauce, mirin, and sugar. Bring to a boil over medium heat, stirring a few times to dissolve the sugar. Reduce the heat to a simmer and cook until it has reduced slightly, 3 to 5 minutes. Remove from the heat, let cool, and transfer the kombu and the liquid to a container with a tight-fitting lid. Store the sweet kombu and "awesome sauce" together in the refrigerator for up to 3 months.

Note You can also start with a 4 × 4-inch piece of dried kombu. Soak the kombu overnight in 4 cups cold water to rehydrate, or cook in a small pot of water over medium heat, turning the heat off right before it boils. The kombu will be soft, pliable, and roughly double its original size. Drain and cut into strips as directed. You can save the soaking water for making Miso Soup (page 41).

Sweet Kombu and Kombu "Awesome Sauce"

昆布の甘煮と
万能昆布ソース

1 piece of kombu leftover
    from making dashi (or
    dried kombu; see Note)
½ cup soy sauce
½ cup mirin
½ cup sugar

Ponzu

ぽん酢

½ cup soy sauce
¼ cup mirin
3 tablespoons yuzu juice or
    strained fresh lemon juice
2 tablespoons rice vinegar
2 tablespoons strained freshly
    squeezed orange juice

This versatile citrusy-soy dipping sauce is something we always have on hand in our refrigerator. It is essential for hotpot (page 149), but also goes great with fried foods and fish because of its acidity.

MAKES ABOUT 1¼ CUPS · TOTAL TIME: 5 MINUTES

In a jar or a storage container with a tight-fitting lid, stir together the soy sauce, mirin, yuzu juice, rice vinegar, and orange juice. Cover and refrigerate until you are ready to use. It can keep for up to 1 month in the refrigerator.

Shiso Pesto

紫蘇ペスト

2 packed cups shiso leaves,
    basil, or a mix of your
    favorite herbs
1 small garlic clove, peeled
6 tablespoons olive oil
¼ teaspoon kosher salt

In the summer, our garden is exploding with fresh shiso, and subbing it in for basil in pesto is just a no-brainer. We love the grassy, floral flavor it brings. If you can't find shiso, a mix of herbs works—obviously basil, but also parsley, mint, chives, or cilantro. We like to double the recipe and freeze some. That way there's always pesto on hand for a quick pasta night, to spread over pizza, or to slather on our Veggie Deluxe Sando (page 106).

MAKES ½ CUP · TOTAL TIME: 5 MINUTES

Bring a small pot of salted water to a boil. Fill a bowl with cold water and ice cubes.

Add the shiso to the boiling water and cook for 15 seconds. Drain, then submerge in the ice bath to chill. Squeeze dry, first with your hands, then in a paper towel to get out as much moisture as possible. Roughly chop and set aside.

In a blender, combine the garlic, olive oil, and salt and blend on high until the garlic is fully blended, about 15 seconds. Add the shiso and blend until bright green and smooth, 15 to 30 seconds. Transfer to a small bowl. Can be stored in an airtight container in the refrigerator for up to 3 days, or in the freezer for up to a month.

Furikake is a mix of seasonings that are sprinkled on top of rice. It comes from two verbs: *Furi* means "shake," and *kakeru* is "pour." Countless varieties can be bought in a Japanese market. The nice thing about making your own is that you know exactly what's in it and can adjust it to your taste. Our son loves putting furikake on his rice. It's his ritual. It's great on onigiri, too (see Furikake Onigiri, page 218). The nori you use should be really fresh and crisp. If it's not, toast it by carefully waving it for a few seconds over an open flame, taking care not to burn it. If the nori isn't fresh, it won't crumble properly when you grind it.

MAKES ⅓ CUP • TOTAL TIME: 5 MINUTES

With a suribachi and surikogi or a mortar and pestle, grind the nori and ½ tablespoon of the salt into a coarse powder. The salt acts as sandpaper and helps grind the nori down. Add the bonito flakes, toasted sesame seeds, and togarashi and pound until coarsely ground. Stir in the remaining ½ tablespoon salt, the sugar, and the aonori, and mix thoroughly. Store in an airtight container in the refrigerator for up to 2 months.

Furikake
Umami Rice Seasoning

ふりかけ

½ sheet nori (about
    4 × 7 inches), torn into
    very small pieces
1 tablespoon flaky sea salt,
    such as Maldon
2 tablespoons bonito flakes
1 tablespoon toasted
    sesame seeds
¼ teaspoon ground
    togarashi, chile flakes,
    or Aleppo pepper
1 teaspoon sugar
1 teaspoon aonori

Breakfast

朝ごはん

While some families mark special mornings with pancakes, our answer to brunch is a full Japanese breakfast. It's our Sunday tradition, a plentiful yet nutritious way to start the day. Japanese breakfast must have rice and miso soup, but from there, we improvise. On weekdays, we keep it simple and add tamagoyaki (a dashi omelet) and tsukemono (Japanese pickles), while on weekends, we go all out with four or five more okazu (foods that are eaten with rice). Pick and choose from the recipes in this chapter to customize your own.

There is no Japanese breakfast without miso soup (pictured on pages 44–45). Give me a small, steaming bowl of soup, some rice and pickles, and I'm ready for the day. Miso soup is my ultimate comfort food. When I have a sip in the morning, I let out a sigh of satisfaction and feel the joy of being alive. It's what I crave the most when I am sick. It's like an elixir.

Miso soup is a simple dish, but you can enhance it with any number of ingredients. In addition to daikon, shiitake, wakame, and tofu, you can add potato and garlic chives, clams and scallions, or kabocha squash and aburaage—whatever appeals to you.

I started making my own miso five years ago, when my son's preschool offered a miso-making class. I like to name it after my kids. It ferments slowly from the cold winter through summer, and the color changes from pale white to light brown, then dark. (Of course, you don't need to make your own.) I like to mix two kinds in my miso soup for depth of flavor, the darker awase and the sweeter saikyo, but it will still be good with just the awase. This recipe makes four small bowls, but if you'd like to make the soup a larger part of your meal, you can easily double it. —**Sawa**

SERVES 4 AS PART OF A LARGER MEAL • TOTAL TIME: 15 MINUTES

Miso Soup

味噌汁

3 cups Dashi (page 33) or
    1 tablespoon dashi powder
    mixed into 3 cups water
2 ounces daikon radish, cut
    into matchsticks
2 large shiitake mushroom
    caps, thinly sliced
1 tablespoon dried wakame
¼ cup awase (blended) miso
1 tablespoon saikyo shiro
    (white) miso
½ cup tofu (silken or
    medium), cut into
    ¼-inch cubes
1 scallion, thinly sliced

In a pot, bring the dashi and daikon to a boil over medium heat. Immediately reduce the heat to low and gently simmer until the daikon turns slightly translucent, about 5 minutes. Add the shiitake mushrooms and cook until soft, about 2 minutes. Add the wakame.

In a small bowl, ladle about ½ cup of the broth over both misos. Use a spoon to loosen the miso and stir it into a thin paste. This will help it dissolve in the soup.

Add the miso-dashi mixture to the pot and stir gently to dissolve. Add the tofu and increase the heat to medium, warming the soup to a steaming-hot serving temperature, taking care not to boil. Ladle into four small bowls, top with the sliced scallions, and serve immediately.

Tamagoyaki

Dashi Rolled Omelet

卵焼き

3 eggs
¼ teaspoon kosher salt
¾ teaspoon sugar
1 tablespoon Dashi
    (page 33) or ⅛ teaspoon
    dashi powder mixed into
    1 tablespoon water
½ teaspoon soy sauce
1 tablespoon canola or other
    neutral oil

Tamagoyaki is a breakfast staple, a sweet-savory rolled omelet flavored with dashi, soy sauce, and a bit of sugar. Our kids like it because it's colorful and easy to eat. We serve it hot out of the pan, but it also travels well. We pack leftovers in our son's bento box for school, or take them on road trips or picnics. Rolling an omelet can seem intimidating, but once you get the hang of it, it's easy. The first roll is the hardest, but if you don't get it right, just power through. The more you roll the omelet, the nicer it will look as you go. There is a specific rectangular pan just for making tamagoyaki that we use at home, but a round nonstick skillet also works.

**SERVES 4 AS PART OF A LARGER MEAL, OR 2 AS THE MAIN EVENT •
TOTAL TIME: 10 MINUTES**

In a bowl or large measuring cup with a pouring spout, whisk together the eggs, salt, sugar, dashi, and soy sauce until fully combined.

Heat an 8-inch nonstick skillet or tamagoyaki pan over medium heat. When a drop of water sprinkled on the surface sizzles, the pan is ready.

Pour in the oil, then wipe out the excess using a paper towel folded into a square, rubbing the pan to lightly coat with oil as you go. Set the paper towel aside for later use.

Pour about one-third of the egg mixture into the pan. It should be hot enough so that the eggs gently sizzle. Using cooking chopsticks or a heat-resistant spatula, immediately push the egg around for a few seconds to coat the bottom of the pan in an even layer. As soon as the egg starts to set but is still wet on top, start rolling at the end of the pan closer to you, using the chopsticks or spatula to fold the edge of the omelet over about 1 inch. Roll that onto itself, pausing to let the egg set before the next roll if necessary. Repeat until you've created a rolled omelet. Once you're finished, slide it back to the end of the pan closer to you. Gently press the roll to flatten a bit and give it an even, rectangular shape with rounded corners.

Working quickly, rub the pan with the oil-soaked paper towel, then pour in just enough egg mixture to coat the bottom of the pan. Swirl the pan to settle the egg in an even layer, making sure that it touches the roll so that they bond. As soon as that layer starts to set but is still wet on top, use the same method to roll the egg to the opposite end of the pan. It will be like a snowball effect—the roll will get fatter as you go. When you have completed the roll, slide the omelet back to the end you started from. Repeat this step until all the liquid egg is used up. Gently press the omelet to flatten a bit using the chopsticks or spatula.

Slide the omelet out of the pan onto a cutting board, seam-side down. Let cool slightly, then slice into ½-inch pieces and serve.

This simple salad is a refreshing accompaniment to breakfast, or really any meal. In the summer, we use Japanese cucumbers (kyuri) from the farmers' market. They are super crispy and a little sweet with a delicate skin so you can eat them unpeeled; and the seeds don't need to be scooped. Other small varieties, like Persian (mini) or Kirby cucumbers, work well, too. You can use English cucumbers in a pinch, but adjust for size, since they're quite big. To thoroughly season the cucumbers, we massage the salt and sugar into the skin, then give them a good smash to break them open, which lets them absorb the flavors of the dressing.

SERVES 4 AS A SIDE DISH • TOTAL TIME: 10 MINUTES

To rehydrate the wakame, soak in a bowl with 2 cups of water for 5 minutes. It will triple or quadruple in size.

Meanwhile, place the cucumbers on a cutting board. Sprinkle with the salt and sugar, and massage into the skin, rolling and rubbing until the exterior is a little moist and some of the salt and sugar has been absorbed (there will be excess salt and sugar on the cutting board, which is okay). Using the side of a chef's knife or the palm of your hand, gently smash the cucumbers, causing them to split open. Cut crosswise into ½-inch pieces (some will break apart into chunks, which is what you're looking for). Transfer to a bowl along with the salt and sugar from the cutting board.

Drain the wakame, squeezing out as much excess water as you can, then blot it with a paper towel. Add to the bowl with the cucumbers and toss a few times with the sesame oil and rice vinegar until everything is coated in dressing. Let sit for about 5 minutes to allow the flavors to meld. Toss again and taste, adding more salt if needed. Transfer to a serving bowl and sprinkle with the toasted sesame seeds. Serve immediately.

Smashed Cucumber and Wakame Salad

叩きキュウリとワカメのサラダ

2 tablespoons dried wakame

2 Japanese, Kirby, or Persian (mini) cucumbers

1½ teaspoons kosher salt, plus more to taste

½ teaspoon sugar

2 teaspoons toasted sesame oil

1 tablespoon plus 1 teaspoon rice vinegar

1 teaspoon toasted sesame seeds

Kinpira

*Braised Burdock Root
and Carrots*

きんぴら

½ cup konnyaku noodles
  or shirataki, cut into
  2½-inch lengths
2 teaspoons toasted
  sesame oil
2 cups finely julienned gobo
  (burdock root), about
  2½ inches long (see Note)
1 cup finely julienned carrot,
  about 2½ inches long
1 small dried togarashi chile,
  seeded, or ½ teaspoon
  chile flakes
2 tablespoons sake
2 tablespoons soy sauce
1 tablespoon mirin
1 tablespoon sugar
½ teaspoon toasted
  sesame seeds

Kinpira (pictured on page 46) is a staple of Japanese households. It's sweet, savory, and earthy, with a toothsome texture from the gobo (burdock root) and a little spice from the togarashi (Japanese chile). It goes well with plain white rice as an okazu, a side dish to accompany rice. We like to make a big pot and eat it over a few days. It tastes better on the second day, as the flavors continue to develop. In addition to being a great breakfast dish, this salad is good to put in a bento box, or to snack on while drinking sake or shochu.

SERVES 4 • TOTAL TIME: 40 MINUTES

Bring a small pot of water to a boil over high heat.

Add the konnyaku noodles and boil for 2 minutes. Drain and set aside.

In a medium pot with a lid, heat the sesame oil over medium heat. Drain the gobo and cook, stirring frequently, until it starts to soften, about 5 minutes. Add the carrot, konnyaku noodles, togarashi, sake, soy sauce, mirin, and sugar and bring to a boil, stirring frequently. Cover, reduce the heat to low, and simmer for 10 minutes, stirring occasionally.

Uncover and continue cooking until most of the liquid has evaporated and the carrots are soft. If serving immediately, transfer to a serving bowl and sprinkle with the toasted sesame seeds. It will keep, covered, in the refrigerator for 4 to 5 days.

Note To clean the gobo, brush it very well with a tawashi or another type of vegetable brush under running water before using. As you cut the gobo into julienne, immediately set them in cold water as you work, to keep them from discoloring.

Hijiki is a type of seaweed that doesn't have a strong taste of its own, so it soaks up whatever you flavor it with. This recipe (pictured on page 45) is a basic braised version seasoned with mirin, sake, soy sauce, and a bit of sugar. My mom made this often, and it showed up in my bento box regularly. Hijiki is low in calories and high in nutrition, so it's good and good for you. Just like wakame and kombu, it comes dried and needs to be soaked in water to rehydrate before cooking. I love eating it braised, like in this recipe, and also added to salad, or cooked in Hijiki and Carrot Rice (page 226). Sometimes I'll add other ingredients, like about ½ cup cooked fish cakes (such as chikuwa, see Fish Cakes on page 155), konnyaku, or atsuage tofu. I cut them in shapes to match the carrots and add them right when the aburaage goes in. —**Sawa**

SERVES 4 AS A SIDE DISH • TOTAL TIME: 40 MINUTES

In a medium bowl, generously cover the hijiki with room-temperature water and let it soak until it has expanded to about eight times its original size (about 2⅔ cups), about 15 minutes. Drain, rinse, and drain again. Set aside.

In a medium pot, heat the olive oil and sesame oil over medium heat just until warm, about 30 seconds. Add the drained hijiki, carrot, and ginger and sauté to cook out any excess water, 2 to 3 minutes. Once you hear the hijiki and carrot start to sizzle, add the sake, mirin, soy sauce, sugar, and aburaage and stir together. Let it come to a boil, then top with a lid one size smaller than the pot you are cooking with, or a plate of similar size, so it fits inside to create a gentle weight. Reduce the heat to low and simmer gently until the carrots are soft and there is about 1 tablespoon of liquid left in the bottom of the pot, 15 to 20 minutes. Add the shelled edamame and mix to incorporate. Discard the ginger.

Transfer to a bowl and serve immediately. Hijiki-ni is also good eaten the next day cold or at room temperature. It will keep, refrigerated, for up to 5 days.

Hijiki-Ni

Braised Hijiki Seaweed

ひじき煮

⅓ cup dried hijiki

2 teaspoons olive oil

1 teaspoon toasted sesame oil

1 cup finely julienned carrot, about 1½ inches long

1 (¼-inch-thick) slice fresh ginger

2 tablespoons sake

1 tablespoon mirin

2 tablespoons soy sauce

1 tablespoon plus 1 teaspoon sugar

1 piece aburaage, halved lengthwise and sliced into ⅛-inch-wide strips

¼ cup fresh or frozen shelled edamame

Spinach Ohitashi

Spinach with Soy Sauce and Bonito Flakes

ほうれん草のお浸し

Salt

1 bunch of spinach
(8 ounces), washed
thoroughly, stems tied
together with butcher's
twine, or 1 (8-ounce)
bag spinach leaves

1 tablespoon dashi shoyu
(see Note)

¼ cup loosely packed
bonito flakes

When I was a kid, spinach always came in bunches. We'd give it a nice bath to wash off the sand. Blanching the spinach was necessary because it tasted bitter when eaten raw. My mom would tie the stems together first so that when she pulled the spinach out of the water, all the stems and leaves would be lined up nicely for when she'd cut them.

Ohitashi means "to soak" or "to steep," and traditional ohitashi entails marinating the spinach for 30 minutes in a dashi and soy mixture. To save time, we omit this step, and drizzle on dashi shoyu, an exceptionally good soy sauce infused with smoky bonito. If you can't find it, regular soy sauce mixed with dashi will work just as well (see Note). —**Sawa**

SERVES 4 • TOTAL TIME: 10 TO 15 MINUTES, DEPENDING ON THE SPINACH YOU USE

Bring a pot of water to a boil and salt it to taste like the sea.

If using a bunch of spinach, place it stem-side first into the boiling water and cook for 1 minute. (If the spinach doesn't fit at first, that's okay—it will wilt and shrink.) Carefully transfer the bunch of spinach using tongs or cooking chopsticks to a small bowl, and run under cold water for about a minute to cool the spinach to room temperature. If using loose spinach leaves, add to the boiling water and cook for 1 minute, then drain in a colander and run under cold water for another minute.

Squeeze the spinach to get as much water out as possible.

Place on a cutting board. If using bunch spinach, remove the string from the bottom end and, starting at the stem end of the bunch, cut across every 2 inches, taking care to keep the little bundles together. If using loose spinach, squeeze together into a log shape approximately 1½ inches wide and cut crosswise in the same way.

Stand up the bundles of spinach and arrange on a serving plate, drizzle with dashi shoyu sauce, top with the bonito flakes, and serve.

Note For a homemade version of dashi shoyu, combine 2 teaspoons high-quality soy sauce with 4 teaspoons dashi, either homemade (page 33) or made by combining ⅛ teaspoon dashi powder with 4 teaspoons water.

Goma is Japanese for "sesame," and *ae* means "tossed together." A version of this dish is made in every Japanese household, and the star is the dressing. It's got a nutty sesame flavor, bolstered with the sweetness of honey, aromatic sake, and a salty hit of soy sauce. The dressing is a lovely match for any raw or simply cooked vegetable. Broccoli is our favorite; the florets act like little mops and hold the sauce beautifully. We also use the stems; the outside is fibrous, but once peeled, it reveals a sweet and tender core. Take care to cut the florets and stem pieces into comparable sizes so they cook evenly. Gomaae broccoli is a staple of our breakfast, but it regularly appears at lunch and dinner, too.

SERVES 4 • TOTAL TIME: 15 MINUTES

Bring a large pot of water to a boil and salt it to taste like the sea.

Cut the broccoli into 1- to 1½-inch florets. Peel the stems and cut into 1- to 1½-inch batons. Set aside.

Coarsely grind the toasted sesame seeds with a suribachi and surikogi (or mortar and pestle, spice grinder, or sesame grinder). Transfer to a medium bowl and mix in the sake, dashi powder, soy sauce, and honey until well combined. Set the bowl of dressing aside.

Add the broccoli florets and stems to the boiling salted water and boil until just cooked through and bright green, about 3 minutes. Drain the broccoli very well, giving it a couple of shakes to remove as much water as possible, then toss with the dressing.

Serve immediately, or store covered in the refrigerator for up to 3 days.

Note Even though we buy already-toasted sesame seeds, we toast them again to intensify their aroma. To do so, place them in a dry skillet over medium heat and toast, stirring often, until golden, about 5 minutes.

Gomaae Broccoli

Broccoli with Sesame Sauce

ブロッコリーの胡麻和え

Salt
1 large head (12 ounces)
    of broccoli
¼ cup toasted sesame seeds,
    toasted once more
    (see Note)
1 tablespoon plus
    1 teaspoon sake
¼ teaspoon dashi powder
2 tablespoons soy sauce
2 teaspoons honey

Shiozake

Broiled Salted Salmon

塩鮭

2 tablespoons kosher salt
1 tablespoon sugar
¼ teaspoon freshly ground
    black pepper
1 (1-pound) skin-on salmon,
    arctic char, or steelhead
    trout fillet, cut into
    4 equal portions

Along with miso soup and rice, this savory salted salmon (pictured on page 44) is a staple of our Japanese breakfast. Curing the salmon extracts excess moisture, which makes the flesh firmer and tastier, while broiling it crisps up the skin. This is a great dish to prepare ahead of time. Once you've salted the salmon, it will keep in the refrigerator for 5 days, or in the freezer for 3 months. We like to have extra shiozake on hand in our freezer for recipes like Salmon and Ikura Rice (page 229), or to just pull out, thaw, and broil whenever we want to eat it. Look for good-quality, naturally farmed or wild-caught salmon.

SERVES 4 • ACTIVE TIME: 20 MINUTES • TOTAL TIME: 12 HOURS OR LONGER FOR CURING THE FISH

In a small bowl, combine the salt, sugar, and black pepper. Place the salmon pieces skin-side down in a single layer in a container with a tight-fitting lid. Sprinkle about two-thirds of the salt mixture onto the flesh side, then flip over the pieces and sprinkle the remaining salt mixture on the skin side. Cover and refrigerate the fish for at least 12 hours and up to 5 days.

When you are ready to cook the fish, position a rack in the center of the oven and preheat the broiler to high. Line a sheet pan with foil.

Remove the fish from the container, pat dry with a paper towel, and brush off the excess salt that hasn't been absorbed. Place the salmon on the lined pan, skin-side up. Broil until the skin starts to bubble and char just a bit and the flesh is just cooked through, 4 to 7 minutes, depending on the thickness of the fillet pieces and how hot the broiler is. Transfer to a platter and serve.

Natto—cooked, fermented soybeans—is a healthy staple of the Japanese breakfast table. Rumor has it that eating it makes you smarter (at least that's what Japanese parents tell their kids). It's funky-smelling like beer, and slimy like okra. Some people are put off by this texture, which the Japanese refer to as neba-neba, but others love it. Although it can be polarizing, natto is still one of the most popular foods in Japan. The way we eat it in our family is a bit unorthodox, mixing in cubed avocado, which adds a creamy texture that goes so well with the neba-neba, almost like a Japanese guacamole. We use special 2 × 4-inch seasoned sheets of nori called ajitsuke-nori to scoop it up, along with some white rice, into our mouths.

We recommend buying natto made with organic or non-GMO soybeans if you can find them. We are big fans of the natto from Kendall Food Company, a small producer in Massachusetts. We also like the more widely available Toromame natto from the Mizkan brand. You'll find it in the refrigerated or frozen section of an Asian grocery store.

SERVES 4 • TOTAL TIME: 10 MINUTES

In a deep serving bowl, combine the natto, soy sauce, aonori, mustard, and scallion. Using a small spoon, vigorously mix until you see the neba-neba start to form. It will look white and airy, like the beans are suspended in a thick spider web, and very slimy. Gently fold in the avocado and serve with ajitsuke-nori and white rice.

Natto with Avocado

アボカド納豆

⅔ cup natto (about three
    50g packages)
2 teaspoons soy sauce
1 teaspoon aonori
1 teaspoon Dijon mustard
1 scallion, thinly sliced
1 avocado, cubed
16 sheets ajitsuke-nori,
    for serving
Japanese White Rice
    (page 215), for serving

Vegetables

野菜

Vegetables are a big part of the Japanese diet; eating seasonally is ingrained in the culture. In Japan, we look beyond the conventional four seasons. There is a different name for each of the many micro seasons, and the bounty of each moment is savored. In Brooklyn, we go to the farmers' market every Saturday. We enjoy looking for that first stalk of asparagus in the spring, or that enormous daikon radish that signifies winter is here. Our meals often include several small dishes of just vegetables, showcasing what is growing nearby.

Much like a classic Caesar dressing, our creamy tofu Caesar dip (pictured on page 60) is zingy and garlicky with a nice dose of umami. Plus, it's vegan—no anchovies or egg yolk here—and it's so easy to make. Just mix the ingredients in a blender. The consistency makes it ideal for dunking, smearing on a sandwich, or drizzling over salad or roasted vegetables. But our favorite method is shoveling it into our mouths as a dip, with a mix of raw and lightly cooked vegetables. Years ago, we taught this recipe to our son's class of four-year-olds, and they loved it. If you want to get your kids to eat their vegetables, give this a try.

SERVES 4 • TOTAL TIME: 15 MINUTES

In a food processor or blender, combine the tofu, soy sauce, vinegar, lemon zest, lemon juice, half of the grated garlic, and the oil. Process or blend on high speed until the ingredients are smooth and combined and look nice and glossy, about 30 seconds. Taste and stir in the other half of the grated garlic if you prefer more. Transfer to a container and taste for seasoning, adding pepper and more soy sauce, if needed. Cover and refrigerate until ready to use.

To serve, place in a bowl and load a platter with your favorite vegetables for dunking. The dip will keep in an airtight container in the refrigerator for up to 4 days.

Tofu Caesar Dip

豆腐シーザーディップ

7 ounces (half of a 14-ounce package) soft or medium-firm tofu, drained
5 teaspoons soy sauce, plus more as needed
1 tablespoon rice vinegar
Grated zest of ½ lemon
1 tablespoon fresh lemon juice (about ½ lemon)
1 small garlic clove, finely grated
¼ cup canola oil
Freshly ground black pepper
Assorted raw vegetables (such as sliced cucumbers, celery, radishes, cherry tomatoes, or bell peppers) and blanched vegetables (like broccoli, asparagus, fava beans, or snow peas), for serving

We love this tangy, zingy carrot-ginger dressing and its vibrant orange color. In the winter we massage it into kale, a sturdy cold-weather green, along with raisins and toasted pumpkin seeds, for a perfectly hearty salad. (Dressed kale is also great when left in the refrigerator overnight to marinate, to be eaten like a slaw the next day.) In the springtime, we douse baby lettuces and radishes with the same dressing, and in the summer, we eat it with larger romaine, along with tomatoes and cucumbers. This is an anytime salad dressing, for any time of year.

SERVES 4 TO 6 • TOTAL TIME: 20 MINUTES

To make the dressing: In a blender, combine the carrot, ginger, vinegar, yuzu juice, honey, soy sauce, and salt and blend on high for 10 seconds. With the blender running, drizzle in the oil and blend until completely smooth. Transfer to a container. The dressing keeps covered for up to 1 week in the refrigerator.

To make the salad: In a small skillet, warm the olive oil over medium heat. Add the pumpkin seeds and toast, stirring frequently, until lightly browned and nutty smelling, 3 to 4 minutes. Season with salt, remove from the pan, and set aside.

In a large bowl, toss the kale with the dressing, massaging it with your hands to thoroughly coat. Sprinkle with the toasted pumpkin seeds, raisins, and grated carrot and serve.

Kale Salad
with Carrot-Ginger Dressing

ケールサラダと
ニンジンドレッシング

Dressing
1 small carrot, cut into rough
    chunks (about ½ cup)
2-inch piece of fresh ginger
2 tablespoons rice vinegar
2 tablespoons yuzu juice
2 tablespoons honey
2 tablespoons soy sauce
1 teaspoon kosher salt
¼ cup canola oil or other
    neutral oil

Salad
1 teaspoon olive oil
¼ cup hulled pumpkin seeds
Kosher salt
8 cups finely shredded Tuscan,
    curly, or Russian red kale,
    midribs removed (about
    2 bunches)
¼ cup golden raisins
¼ cup grated carrot
    (grated on the large
    holes of a box grater)

Tomato and Tofu Salad

with Umeboshi

梅干し入り豆腐トマトサラダ

10 ounces medium-firm tofu

3 tablespoons smashed
(into a paste) pitted
umeboshi plums

1 tablespoon soy sauce

2 tablespoons olive oil

2 large heirloom tomatoes,
cored and cut into slices
or wedges

4 large shiso leaves, torn
into pieces

If a tomato wanted to cheat on basil, it would run away with shiso. Shiso has all of the floral, herbaceous qualities of basil but with its own unique, delicate taste. Come summer, when we have a garden bursting with shiso and a counter full of ripe tomatoes, we like to put them together in what is basically a Japanese vegan caprese—with tofu standing in for the mozzarella. And instead of using an acid in the dressing, we use umeboshi, which are salted and fermented plums with a complex, salty-sour-sweet taste. In Japan, umeboshi are considered a health food, with all sorts of restorative properties. Eat them in the summer when you're hot and exhausted, and the bracing flavor perks you right up.

SERVES 4 • TOTAL TIME: 15 MINUTES

Wrap the tofu in a paper towel. Place it on a plate and put a small plate on top of the tofu. Let it sit for 10 minutes. This will help press out any excess liquid.

Meanwhile, to make the dressing, combine the umeboshi paste, soy sauce, and olive oil in a small bowl and mix together thoroughly. It will be thick. It's okay if the dressing is broken and not fully emulsified.

Place the tomatoes on a large serving platter. Unwrap the tofu and, using your hands, gently tear it into 1- to 2-inch chunks. Intersperse the tofu among the tomato wedges. Spoon the dressing over and around the tomatoes and tofu. Sprinkle on the torn shiso and serve.

Eating shishito peppers is kind of like playing Russian roulette: About one in ten is spicy. As the season turns to fall, a higher percentage of the peppers are spicy, and the spice level gets higher. If you're like our son and don't like heat, early summer is a great time to get shishitos from the market, when they tend to be milder. Regardless, he loves them, so he nibbles the end of each pepper to check if it's hot (the tip is always less spicy since there are fewer seeds at the end of a pepper). If it is, he passes it to us. If not, he scarfs it down.

Flavored salts, like citrusy, herby shiso-lime salt, can elevate even simple preparations such as this one. It's easy to make and so versatile. We love having a jarful in our refrigerator all summer long to sprinkle on raw and grilled vegetables.

SERVES 4 · TOTAL TIME: 15 MINUTES

Pulverize the shiso and 1 tablespoon of the salt together with a suribachi and surikogi (or a mortar and pestle) until the shiso is broken down and the salt is green. (Alternatively, put the shiso on a cutting board, mix with the salt, and use a large knife to rock back and forth and chop the salt and shiso together.) The salt will act like sandpaper and help to further break down the shiso.

Put the salt-shiso mixture into a small bowl. Add the remaining 1 tablespoon salt, the sugar, and lime zest and mix together. Set aside. The shiso-lime salt will keep covered in the refrigerator for up to 1 month.

Heat a yakiami, grill pan, or cast-iron skillet over high heat until it is very hot and just starting to smoke. Toss the shishito peppers in a large bowl with the oil.

Working in batches, place peppers in a single layer on the yakiami or in the pan, taking care not to overcrowd them. Cook until the skin starts to blister and brown, 1 to 2 minutes. Flip and cook until the other side is blistered and the peppers have softened just a bit, 1 to 2 minutes. Transfer to a serving plate and repeat with the remaining peppers.

Sprinkle the shiso-lime salt over the peppers, or serve it in a small side dish for individual dipping.

Blistered Shishito Peppers
with Shiso-Lime Salt

焼ししとうと紫蘇ライムソルト

3 shiso leaves, finely chopped
2 tablespoons kosher or coarse
    sea salt
2 teaspoons sugar
Grated zest of 1 lime
1 pound shishito peppers
1 teaspoon canola or other
    neutral oil

Japanese Street Corn

焼とうもろこし

Kosher salt or sea salt
4 ears corn, shucked
Olive oil, for brushing
Kewpie mayonnaise,
    for drizzling
¼ cup grated Cotija cheese
A few pinches of shichimi
    togarashi
2 scallions, thinly sliced
1 lime, cut into 4 to 6 wedges

This dish is inspired by elote, Mexican street corn, which is dressed with mayo and sprinkled with chile and Cotija cheese, then spritzed with fresh lime. For our Japanese-style version, we use Kewpie mayo and shichimi togarashi, because we love luxuriously rich Kewpie mayo, and the complexity of the seven different spices in shichimi togarashi. (For a healthier version, sub in our Tofu Caesar Dip, page 59, for the mayo.)

To get plenty of seasoning on all sides of the corn, after parboiling them we cut the ears into several wedges before grilling, a technique that ensures every bite is loaded with goodness. We recommend using a sharp serrated knife (and lots of care) to saw through the cobs. If you'd rather keep the corn whole, it will still be delicious.

SERVES 4 TO 6 • TOTAL TIME: 20 MINUTES

Bring a large pot of water to a boil over high heat and salt it to taste like the sea. Add the corn and cook for 5 minutes. Remove from the pot and set aside on a cutting board.

Once the corn is cool enough to handle, cut each ear of corn in half crosswise. Stand one half up on the cut end and slice through the center of the cob lengthwise. Lay the two pieces flat side down and split each one again lengthwise, so you have four equal wedges. Repeat with the remaining corn. You should end up with 32 wedges.

Brush the kernel side of the corn wedges very lightly with olive oil and sprinkle with salt to season.

Heat a grill, grill pan, or yakiami over high heat. Grill the corn wedges, kernel-side down, until the kernels are charred just a bit, 2 to 3 minutes (the corn is already cooked, so you're just looking to get some nice smoky flavor). Cook in batches, fitting as many wedges of corn as you can without crowding.

Place the grilled corn on a large serving platter with the kernel side facing up. Generously drizzle with the Kewpie mayo, and sprinkle with the Cotija cheese, shichimi togarashi, and scallions. Serve with the lime wedges to squeeze on just before eating.

Smashed Satoimo

潰し里芋のお焼き

2 pounds egg-size taro roots
(about 8 taro)
2 tablespoons kosher salt,
plus more for sprinkling
1 cup cornstarch
Canola oil or other neutral
oil, for shallow-frying
2 scallions, thinly sliced
½ cup finely grated daikon
radish
Ponzu (page 36), for serving

In Japanese, taro is called satoimo. Similar to the taro you see in Hawaii, Japanese satoimo are smaller and more slippery when peeled. They reveal beautiful white flesh after losing their dirty, fuzzy skin. When cooked, these are sweeter, creamier, and denser than potatoes. The typical way to prepare satoimo is to braise them or put them in soups, but we like to boil, smash, and fry them for an instant crowd-pleaser. Taro can be found in many Asian grocery stores, but similar sizes of potato, such as Yukon Gold, Red Bliss, or fingerlings are all good substitutes.

SERVES 4 • ACTIVE TIME: 1 HOUR • TOTAL TIME: 2 HOURS

In a large pot, combine the taro, salt, and enough water to cover by 2 inches. Bring to a boil over high heat. Reduce to a simmer and cook until a cake tester or tip of a small knife can be inserted easily, anywhere from 45 minutes to 1 hour. Drain and let cool slightly, then, using a small knife, peel the taro while still warm. (If they are too cool, they will be difficult to peel.) Refrigerate to cool completely.

Using the palm of your hand, smash each taro into a patty about ½ inch thick. Smaller taro are easier to work with, so if any are larger than an egg, cut them in half before smashing. It's okay if the edges get a little broken and cracked—this translates to crispy edges when fried. At this stage, you can store the taro in the refrigerator for up to 3 days before frying.

Place the smashed taro in an even layer on a baking sheet. Put the cornstarch in a small fine-mesh sieve and dust a fine layer over the taro to cover completely. Flip and repeat with the other side.

Set the oven to its lowest temperature. Line a baking sheet with paper towels.

In a large skillet, heat about ¼ inch canola oil over medium heat. Test the oil by sprinkling in a little cornstarch. If it starts to sizzle, it's ready.

Add as many taro as you can fit in a single layer without crowding the pan. Fry until golden brown, gently swirling the pan to help them cook evenly, 6 to 8 minutes. Flip and fry the other side until golden brown, 4 to 6 minutes. Transfer to the lined baking sheet and sprinkle with salt. Repeat with the remaining taro. Keep the fried taro warm in the oven until ready to serve.

Transfer the taro to a serving platter. Place the scallions, grated daikon, and ponzu in three small bowls. Place a few taro on your plate, then spoon grated daikon on top, sprinkle with some scallions, and drizzle with ponzu.

In Japanese cooking, it's common to pair eggplant with atsuage tofu, a deep-fried tofu that's not crispy but has skin with a little chew that helps hold the tofu together while it simmers. Like the eggplant, the tofu acts as a sponge, soaking in liquid while keeping its shape. With the sweet-savory combination of soy, mirin, sake, and dashi, this dish just hits the spot. It's a little saucy, which makes it great with rice, and is good eaten hot or cold. You can find atsuage tofu with the other tofu varieties at a Japanese or Asian grocer, where it's sometimes labeled "fried tofu cutlet." If you can't find it, medium-firm tofu is a good substitute.

SERVES 4 • TOTAL TIME: 30 MINUTES

Halve the eggplants lengthwise. Lay the pieces cut-side down on the cutting board. Score the skin at a 45-degree angle, making shallow cuts about ⅛ inch deep and spaced ¼ inch apart. Fully cut through every ¾ inch, so you have ¾-inch-thick diagonal pieces with 2 scores in each one. This will tenderize the skin and help the eggplant absorb the liquid.

In a medium pot with a lid, bring the sake and mirin to a boil over high heat to cook off the alcohol, about 2 minutes. Add the soy sauce, salt, sugar, and dashi and bring back to a boil. Put the eggplant and tofu in the pot and return to a boil. Reduce the heat to low, cover, and simmer, gently stirring once or twice, until the eggplant is fork-tender and the flesh has turned darker from the soy braising liquid, 10 to 12 minutes.

In a small bowl, mix the cornstarch and the 4 teaspoons water to make a slurry. Uncover the pot, pour the slurry all around the simmering pot and add the ginger. Stir gently so as not to break apart the delicate tofu or eggplant, and simmer until the sauce thickens just a bit and everything is nicely glazed, 30 seconds to 1 minute.

Serve in a shallow bowl with the scallions sprinkled on top.

Simmered Japanese Eggplant
with Atsuage Tofu

茄子と厚揚げの煮物

2 Japanese eggplants
   (about 8 inches long)
¼ cup sake
¼ cup mirin
2 tablespoons soy sauce
½ teaspoon kosher salt
2 teaspoons sugar
1 cup Dashi (page 33) or
   1 teaspoon dashi powder
   mixed into 1 cup water
12 ounces atsuage tofu
   (fried tofu), cut into
   ½-inch cubes
4 teaspoons cornstarch
4 teaspoons water
1½ teaspoons finely grated
   fresh ginger
1 scallion, thinly sliced, or a
   few sprigs mitsuba, torn

Cauliflower is a perfect canvas for our miso and panko butter. The aged flavor of the miso combined with butter creates a flavor that reminds us of a complex cheddar or parmesan cheese, and the panko binds it all together into a delicious topping. As good as it is on the cauliflower, it's just as tasty on a variety of things, be it other vegetables, roasted fish, scallops, or chicken breasts. You can make the butter in larger batches and store in the freezer, where it will keep for months.

SERVES 4 • TOTAL TIME: 40 MINUTES

Preheat the oven to 400°F. Line a baking sheet with parchment paper or foil.

In a small bowl, mix together the butter, miso, and panko until the ingredients form a paste. Set aside.

Brush the cauliflower wedges with olive oil and season all over with the salt and a few cracks of black pepper. Lay, flat-side down, on the prepared baking sheet, leaving a little space between the pieces. Slide into the oven and roast until the bottom side is nicely caramelized, about 20 minutes.

Using a spoon or spatula, flip the wedges and press on the butter in a thin layer, covering as much of the surface as you can. Roast until the miso-panko butter has turned a deep golden brown and the cauliflower is cooked through, 10 to 15 minutes.

Remove from the oven and transfer to a serving platter. Serve immediately, with lemon wedges on the side for squeezing.

Roasted Cauliflower
with Miso and Panko Butter

カリフラワーの味噌パン粉バター

4 tablespoons unsalted butter, at room temperature
2 tablespoons awase (blended) miso or aka (red) miso
3 tablespoons panko bread crumbs
1 head cauliflower (about 1¼ pounds), leaves trimmed, cut into 8 wedges
2 tablespoons olive oil
½ teaspoon kosher salt
Freshly ground black pepper
4 lemon wedges

Roasted Satsumaimo
with Shio Koji Butter

焼き芋と塩麹バター

4 Japanese sweet potatoes,
　　washed
8 tablespoons (1 stick)
　　unsalted butter, cubed,
　　at room temperature
3 tablespoons shio koji

In the neighborhood I grew up in, a little truck selling sweet potatoes would go around playing a song on a speaker, *ishi yaki imo*, or "rock-baked potato," over and over again. So naturally I'd start thinking, let's grab an ishi yaki imo. They give it to you in a newspaper bag, still super warm so it heats your hands while you eat it. It's slow-roasted over rocks, which coaxes out a sweetness you can't get at home. We'd often put butter on it and have it just like that.

Though we can't re-create the rock-baked flavor of ishi yaki imo at home, this recipe stirs up those memories. We wash the sweet potatoes and wrap them in wet newspaper and foil, to keep them moist. Slow-baking is the key, as you want the potatoes to be tender and sweet. Shio koji butter balances that sweetness while packing a wallop of umami. If you have extra shio koji butter, it freezes well. It's wonderful with other vegetables, like potatoes and carrots, or sweet corn in the summer months. **—Sawa**

SERVES 4 • ACTIVE TIME: 10 MINUTES • TOTAL TIME: 2 HOURS

Preheat the oven to 350°F.

Fill a large bowl with water. Submerge 4 pieces of newspaper for 30 seconds. Remove from the water and wrap each sweet potato tightly in wet newspaper, then cover and tightly wrap with foil. Bake until completely soft, 1½ to 2 hours. To test if the potatoes are ready, squeeze them gently (no need to unwrap). If they feel soft and give easily, they're done.

While the potatoes are baking, put the butter in a small bowl. Whisk in the shio koji 1 teaspoon at a time, making sure each addition is incorporated before adding the next, until all of the koji is mixed in.

Unwrap the cooked potatoes, split them in half lengthwise, and serve while still warm, with the shio koji butter on the side. Spoon as much butter onto each potato as you'd like and enjoy.

This is a perfect recipe for autumn and winter, when our favorite squash is in season. Kabocha squash is sweet, starchy, dense, and packed with nutrients. In this dish, the vegetable is the star, and the pork is the garnish. The hearty sauce is a salty, meaty foil to kabocha's sweetness, and it coats the creamy squash beautifully. This can be a satisfying side or an entrée—just add miso soup and rice to make it a meal. This recipe works well with other ground meat, such as chicken or beef.

SERVES 4 AS A MAIN COURSE • TOTAL TIME: 45 MINUTES

Set up a steamer basket or a metal colander in a large pot with a lid. Add enough water to the pot so that it comes just under the basket. Put the kabocha wedges in a bowl and sprinkle with 1 teaspoon of the kosher salt and toss to coat the pieces evenly. Arrange the wedges in the basket without overlapping, re-creating the shape of the whole squash as best as you can, so that the pieces cook evenly. Cover the pot, bring the water to a boil over medium-high heat, and steam until the squash is soft but not falling apart, about 15 minutes. A cake tester or thin knife inserted into the squash should glide in easily. Transfer to a serving bowl and set aside.

To make the meat sauce, heat a large skillet over high heat. (If the pork is lean or if using lean meats such as poultry, heat the pan with 1 tablespoon oil.) Add the ground pork and break up the meat with a wooden spoon. Cook until it starts to brown, about 5 minutes, then reduce the heat to medium and cook for another 5 minutes.

Add the onion, garlic, and ginger and cook until the onion becomes soft, 7 to 10 minutes. Add the sake and mirin and bring to a boil to cook off the alcohol. Add the soy sauce and ½ cup of the water and bring back to a boil. Taste and add the remaining teaspoon of salt, a few cracks of black pepper, and the sugar.

In a small bowl, mix the cornstarch with the remaining 2 tablespoons water to make a slurry. Pour the slurry into the meat sauce and return to a boil, stirring constantly. When the sauce is thickened and glossy, pour it over the kabocha and serve.

Kabocha Squash
with Meat Sauce

かぼちゃの肉味噌あんかけ

1 kabocha squash (1½ to 2 pounds), seeded and cut into 8 equal wedges
2 teaspoons kosher salt
1 pound ground pork
1 tablespoon canola or other neutral oil (optional)
1 yellow onion, diced
2 garlic cloves, minced
1½ teaspoons grated fresh ginger
¼ cup sake
¼ cup mirin
3 tablespoons soy sauce
½ cup plus 2 tablespoons water
Freshly ground black pepper
¼ teaspoon sugar
1½ tablespoons cornstarch

Pancakes and Friends

大勢で楽しむ料理

This is a chapter about fun food, inspired by what you might find at an izakaya, the Japanese equivalent of a pub, or at a street stall in an alleyway in Japan. These recipes are some combination of starchy, stuffed, or fried, equal parts food and snack. They like to be dunked or slathered in sauces, or have bonito flakes dancing on top, and are often oozing with melted cheese. They can be eaten with your hands, and demand a cold beer. These are our party foods, and you'll find they require at least two napkins to enjoy.

There are many types of okonomiyaki in Japan, and each region has its own unique version. But since I grew up in Hiroshima, the one I hold dear is Hiroshima-style: a layered pancake consisting of a crepe-like batter, a mound of cabbage, bean sprouts, sliced pork, crispy ramen noodles, and a fried egg. It's labor-intensive, as they are added one at a time and slowly cooked, so I came up with this cheat version that I make at home. The method requires some multitasking with two frying pans, but it's easier than it sounds. —**Sawa**

SERVES 4 TO 6 • TOTAL TIME: 1½ HOURS

To make the okonomiyaki: In a bowl, mix the all-purpose flour, rice flour, salt, sugar, and baking soda until well combined. Pour in the dashi and whisk until just incorporated. Just like any pancake batter, it can be a bit lumpy. Don't overmix.

Add the cabbage, bean sprouts, and onion and mix by hand until the vegetables are distributed evenly in the batter. (You can make the batter up to a day in advance. Before cooking, pour any liquid off the top that was released from the vegetables, taking care not to pour out the batter.)

Bring a large pot of water to a boil.

Drop in the ramen noodles, stir immediately, and cook according to the package directions (see How to Cook Japanese Noodles, page 124). Drain and run under cold water until chilled. Drain thoroughly, then place in a bowl and toss with a splash of canola oil so they don't stick together. Divide into four equal portions and set aside.

Set the oven to its lowest temperature. Line a sheet pan with foil or set a cooling rack in the pan.

Set two 8-inch cast-iron or other nonstick pans on your stove. Heat one pan over medium heat and add 2 tablespoons canola oil. Add 1 cup of the okonomiyaki batter and spread into a round, even pancake about 6 inches across and ½ inch thick. Cook until the edges start to brown, 3 to 4 minutes. Add 2 slices of the pork belly on top in an even layer. Using a spatula, flip the okonomiyaki and cook for another 2 minutes, until just set and very lightly golden.

Hiroshima-Style Okonomiyaki
with Ramen Noodles

広島風お好み焼き

Okonomiyaki
1 cup all-purpose flour
¼ cup rice flour
2 teaspoons kosher salt
2 teaspoons sugar
¼ teaspoon baking soda
1 cup chilled Dashi (page 33) or 1 teaspoon dashi powder mixed into 1 cup cold water
2 cups tightly packed finely shredded green cabbage
2 cups bean sprouts
1 cup thinly sliced onion

12 ounces fresh ramen noodles (3 ounces for each okonomiyaki)
Canola oil, for pan-frying
8 slices thinly sliced pork belly or bacon, cut in half
4 eggs
Okonomi sauce, homemade (page 34) or store-bought (we like Otafuku brand)
Kewpie mayonnaise, for drizzling
2 scallions, thinly sliced
1 teaspoon aonori
Bonito flakes, for sprinkling

continued

PANCAKES AND FRIENDS

Working quickly, in the second pan, heat ¼ teaspoon oil over medium heat. Add a portion of the ramen noodles and spread into a round, even patty about 6 inches across, the same size as the okonomiyaki. Using a spatula, lift the okonomiyaki out of the first pan and place on top of the noodle patty. Turn the heat to the lowest setting to slowly crisp up the noodles, then move to the next step to cook your egg in the just-emptied pan.

Wipe out the pan if necessary, add a little more oil if needed, then warm over medium heat. Crack an egg into it and turn the heat to low. After it sizzles for a few seconds, use a spatula to break the yolk and spread it all over the pan to about the same size as the okonomiyaki. Before the egg fully sets, use a spatula to lift the okonomiyaki and place directly on top of the egg, noodle-side down. Cook for a minute, so the egg cooks and binds with the noodles.

Put a plate that is larger than the okonomiyaki over the pan, then invert the okonomiyaki, egg-side up, onto the plate. Transfer to the prepared baking sheet and place in the oven. Repeat three more times with the remaining ingredients to make all 4 okonomiyaki.

To serve, put an okonomiyaki, egg-side up, on each of four plates. Brush on a thin layer of the okonomi sauce. Drizzle with Kewpie mayo, and sprinkle with the scallions, aonori, and bonito flakes. Serve immediately.

Variation:

KANSAI-STYLE OKONOMIYAKI:

From the region that encompasses Osaka, this version is simpler than the Hiroshima-style. The okonomiyaki batter is the same, and you'll only need one pan. Omit the ramen noodles and the egg. After cooking the first side of the pancake, put on the pork belly, flip, and cook the second side until crispy, 4 to 5 minutes. Flip again and crisp the other side for 1 minute. Remove from the pan and repeat with the remaining batter and pork belly. Top with the okonomi sauce, Kewpie mayo, scallions, aonori, and bonito flakes, and serve.

Nagaimo-Ika Yaki

Japanese Mountain Yam and Squid Pancake

長芋イカ焼き

12 ounces nagaimo
2 teaspoons dashi powder
1 teaspoon kosher salt
1 egg
¼ cup cornstarch
2 tablespoons all-purpose
    flour (or rice flour for
    gluten-free)
5 scallions, thinly sliced
4 ounces cleaned squid,
    bodies sliced into
    thin rings
Canola or another neutral
    oil, for shallow-frying
Soy sauce or Ponzu (page 36),
    for dipping

Nagaimo, also known as Japanese mountain yam, has a wet texture that is almost slimy, or neba-neba in Japanese. It has a neutral flavor and is commonly eaten grated raw over rice or noodles with a drizzle of soy sauce. But it's also wonderful cooked in dishes like these savory pancakes. When you fry the nagaimo the sliminess goes away, and the moisture makes the pancake tender and light. It's easy and quick to put this dish together, and it's good for appetizers or a light lunch. If you like, you can use shrimp or scallops instead of squid. Nagaimo is sold in most Asian grocery stores. It is very slippery when peeled, so be careful when grating. Wrapping the nagaimo with a paper towel helps you get a firmer grip.

MAKES 8 TO 10 SMALL PANCAKES (SERVES 4) • TOTAL TIME: 40 MINUTES

Line a sheet pan with paper towels and set aside.

Peel the nagaimo and grate on the fine holes of a box grater. It will become liquidy and a bit slimy when grated. Transfer to a bowl.

Add the dashi powder, salt, and egg, and mix until fully incorporated. Using a rubber spatula, fold in the cornstarch, flour, scallions, and squid until the flour and cornstarch are no longer visible. Set aside.

Pour ¼ inch canola oil into a large heavy-bottomed sauté pan or cast-iron skillet and warm over medium heat. Test the temperature of the oil by sprinkling in a few drops of batter. If it starts to sizzle immediately, the oil is ready for frying.

Stir the batter once or twice, then scoop ¼ cup into the pan. Using the back of a spoon, spread evenly until about ⅓ inch thick and 3 inches across, the size of a silver dollar pancake. Stir the batter before scooping and repeat until you've filled the skillet, leaving a little space between the pancakes.

Cook until the sides start to turn golden brown, about 3 minutes. Flip and cook until the other side turns golden brown, about 3 minutes longer. If the pancakes are getting too dark, reduce the heat. If they're too pale, leave for another minute and slightly increase the heat. Remove from the skillet and place on the lined baking sheet to drain. Repeat with the remaining batter.

Serve immediately with soy sauce or ponzu dipping sauce on the side.

Aburaage is fried tofu skin that also happens to be a perfect pocket-like vessel for stuffing. Our recipe is inspired by the cheese-filled aburaage in one of our favorite cookbooks, *Izakaya* by Mark Robinson. We built onto that base by adding ham, but experiment with your favorite fillings—this snack is perfect for kids, and happens to be gluten-free, too.

Aburaage is available in the tofu or freezer section of Japanese or Asian markets, and usually comes in a few shapes and sizes. For this recipe, we call for rectangular aburaage that measures 2½ × 5 inches, which we cut in half to make square pouches. If you can only find larger aburaage, just put a bit more stuffing in each one.

SERVES 4 • TOTAL TIME: 20 MINUTES

Preheat the oven to 400°F. Line a baking sheet with foil or parchment paper.

Gently open the aburaage at the cut end and stuff with a piece of ham and some cheese, dividing them evenly among the pouches. Use a toothpick to close up the cut ends, threading it through the aburaage two times. Place spaced apart on the baking sheet.

Bake until the aburaage take on a slightly more golden-brown color and get a little crispy, 7 to 9 minutes, flipping the pockets over halfway through. The cheese should be melted, but not so hot that it comes oozing out. Serve straight from the oven.

Ham and Cheese–Stuffed Aburaage

ハムチーズ入り油揚げ

Four 2½ × 5-inch pieces aburaage, halved to make eight 2½-inch squares
2 slices ham, quartered
6 ounces cheddar cheese or your favorite melting cheese, roughly chopped

Variations:

MUSHROOM AND FONTINA–STUFFED ABURAAGE:
Substitute fontina cheese for the cheddar and reduce to 4 ounces. Thinly slice 7 shiitake mushroom caps (or an equivalent amount of your favorite mushroom). Sauté the sliced mushrooms in olive oil over medium heat until lightly browned, 3 to 4 minutes. Stuff 1 tablespoon of the cooked mushrooms into each pocket along with the cheese.

PIZZA–POCKET ABURAAGE:
Substitute mozzarella for the cheddar and put a tablespoonful of tomato sauce and a fresh basil leaf into each pocket.

SWISS ALPS–STYLE ABURAAGE:
Substitute raclette for the cheddar and reduce to 4 ounces. Stuff a halved cornichon and a slice or two of boiled peeled fingerling potato into each pocket. Serve with Dijon mustard.

Sawa's mom's harumaki were the first thing I ever ate in Japan, on my first visit to her parents. I was totally jet-lagged, but when I got to their apartment in Hiroshima, a heaping plate of freshly fried harumaki was promptly placed on the table. Sawa's dad started pouring shochu. From that moment on, I knew my life had taken a turn, and I was in for an amazing experience. The harumaki were thin, crispy wrappers filled with juicy pork, mushrooms, lots of scallions, and earthy bamboo, all sliced into remarkably thin strips for an elegant texture. A soy-vinegar dipping sauce cut through the richness. The hospitality revived me, even if the shochu put me to sleep. I'm so thankful Sawa's mom shared her recipe with us. It was Sawa's special request, and having eaten them, I understand why. —**Aaron**

SERVES 4 TO 6 · ACTIVE TIME: 2 HOURS · TOTAL TIME: 3 HOURS

To make the dipping sauce: In a small bowl, combine the soy sauce and vinegar. This can be done in advance and will keep indefinitely in the refrigerator.

To make the filling: In a heatproof container with a lid, combine the mushrooms and sugar. Pour in 1 cup of the boiling water, cover, and let sit for 30 minutes. Once the mushrooms are plump and rehydrated, remove them from the liquid. Discard the stems and thinly slice the caps, then return to the soaking liquid and set aside.

In a heatproof bowl, cover the rice vermicelli with the remaining 2 cups boiling water. Let sit for 3 minutes until rehydrated. Drain the water and set the noodles aside. Once cool, use a pair of scissors to snip the noodles a few times so they are not too long and roughly bite-size. It doesn't have to be precise.

In a wok or a large skillet, heat the canola oil over high heat until very hot. Add the pork and cook, stirring occasionally, until it starts to brown, 6 to 8 minutes. Add the salt, scallion whites, and ginger and cook, stirring frequently until the scallions have just softened, 1 to 2 minutes. Add the bamboo and cook for another 1 to 2 minutes, stirring occasionally. Add the sake and cook until it has completely reduced and there is no liquid in the pan. Add the shiitake and their soaking liquid and the scallion greens. Cook until the scallion tops have softened, 2 to 3 minutes. Add the chicken stock and soy sauce and bring to a boil.

continued

Harumaki

Sawa's Mama's Spring Rolls

母の春巻

Dipping Sauce
2 tablespoons soy sauce
2 tablespoons black vinegar
  or rice vinegar

Filling
12 dried shiitake mushrooms
1 tablespoon sugar
3 cups boiling water
1¼ ounces dried rice vermicelli
2 teaspoons canola or
  vegetable oil
12 ounces boneless pork
  shoulder, cut into thin strips
  2 inches long
2 teaspoons kosher salt
2 bunches scallions, white
  part thinly sliced on the
  diagonal, green part cut into
  2-inch lengths
2 tablespoons minced fresh
  ginger
1 cup finely julienned bamboo
  shoots (from an 8-ounce can
  or 5-ounce Cryovaced piece)
¼ cup sake
½ cup chicken stock (or Dashi,
  page 33, or ½ teaspoon
  dashi powder mixed into
  ½ cup water)
1 teaspoon soy sauce
2 tablespoons cornstarch
2 tablespoons cold water

Spring Rolls
16 spring roll wrappers (8-inch
  squares), such as Spring
  Home or Ryushobo brand
Canola or vegetable oil,
  for shallow-frying

In a small bowl, mix the cornstarch with the cold water to make a slurry. Add the slurry to the filling while stirring constantly, and continue cooking until the pork and vegetables are coated in a thick sauce, 30 seconds to 1 minute. Remove from the heat and transfer the filling to a bowl. Let sit for 5 to 10 minutes to cool down a bit, then mix in the rice vermicelli, stirring to incorporate. Refrigerate and let cool completely, then cover. The filling can be made up to 3 days in advance.

To make the spring rolls: Prepare a work surface with the filling, the spring roll wrappers, and a damp towel to cover the wrappers when you're not using them, to prevent them from drying out. Position a wrapper with a corner facing you. Put ¼ cup of filling in the lower third of the wrapper, and shape it into a log that almost reaches the edges. Fold the corner facing you over the filling, then roll toward the center. Stop at the center, fold the left and right corners inward, then finish rolling. (You want it on the tighter side, but not so tight that it will split when frying.) Set on a plate, seam-side down, and continue with the remaining wrappers. It should make 16 harumaki.

Set the oven to its lowest temperature. Line a sheet pan with paper towels and set a cooling rack into the pan to drain the fried spring rolls (the rack will keep the bottoms crispy).

Pour ½ inch canola oil into a large cast-iron skillet or another heavy-duty pan. Set the skillet over medium-high heat and warm until shimmering, about 350°F on a deep-fry thermometer. Gently lay a harumaki in the pan, seam-side down. You should be able to fit 3 or 4 pieces at a time without them touching or overcrowding. Cook until the bottom half is golden brown, 1 to 1½ minutes. Using tongs or cooking chopsticks, flip them over and cook until the other side is golden brown, another 1 to 1½ minutes. You only need to get the wrapper crispy and golden brown, since the filling is already cooked. Set on the rack in the sheet pan and transfer to the oven to keep warm. Repeat with the remaining harumaki.

Serve hot with the dipping sauce on the side.

Some years back when we were visiting Kamakura, a beautiful beach town in Kanagawa prefecture, we went to a pizza restaurant, sat on the terrace, had a glass of wine, and ordered a chrysanthemum pizza (shungiku in Japanese). We'd never thought about putting this grassy and floral green on a pizza before. It was incredible.

Later, when we started making pizza at home, we remembered our meal in Kamakura. In addition to putting chrysanthemum greens on top (you can get them in Asian markets), bamboo shoots are another favorite. They have a subtle nutty flavor, and remain firm even after cooking, a nice contrast with the sauce and gooey cheese. Though fresh bamboo shoots are hard to find, the next best thing are the blanched, vacuum-sealed ones from Japanese grocers. If using the canned variety, rinse them first to minimize the metallic taste.

Our dough, which is naturally leavened with the starter for our Rakkenji Shokupan (page 102), is pretty easy to work with. We always weigh our ingredients when making dough because a scale is more precise than a cup measure, especially when dealing with flour. Once you get it in the containers to rise, it can keep in the fridge for up to 5 days, so you can make the dough on Wednesday for your Saturday pizza party.

SERVES 4 OR 5 • ACTIVE TIME: 1 HOUR • TOTAL TIME: 5 HOURS

To make the dough: In the bowl of a stand mixer or a large mixing bowl, combine the starter, water, flour, sugar, and salt. If using a stand mixer, mix with the dough hook attachment on low speed for 5 to 7 minutes. If mixing manually, mix with a wooden spoon until it comes together in a sticky dough.

When the dough is one big mass, wet your hands and shape it into a ball. The dough will be sticky and wet. Cover the bowl with a lid or a plastic wrap and let sit for 30 minutes at room temperature for the first fermentation.

Uncover and wet your hands. Gently reach under the dough ball, pull up one side and fold it over and toward the center. Repeat with the three remaining sides, then cover the bowl and let it sit for another 30 minutes.

Repeat the previous step, let sit for 30 minutes, then repeat once more for 3 total folds and let sit for another 30 minutes. The dough should look silky and stretchy. If it's not, add 1 to 2 tablespoons of flour and knead well. Then cover and let sit for another 30 minutes.

continued

PANCAKES AND FRIENDS

89

Japanese Garden Pizza

春菊と筍の楽健寺ピザ

Pizza Dough

100g (½ cup) ripe Rakkenji Starter (page 99)

375g (1½ cups) lukewarm water

600g (4¾ cups) all-purpose flour

Pinch of sugar

10g (1 tablespoon) kosher salt

4 tablespoons olive oil, plus more as needed

Cooking spray

Semolina, for dusting

Toppings

1 cup tomato sauce

¼ cup bamboo shoots (vacuum-sealed or canned), quartered and thinly sliced

2 scallions, thinly sliced

1 large ball (about 8 ounces) fresh mozzarella, sliced thin or grated on the large holes of a box grater

½ bunch chrysanthemum greens, washed and dried, hard stems removed, cut into 2-inch pieces

Kosher salt, for sprinkling

Uncover the bowl and wet your hands. Gently reach under the dough ball, pull up one side and fold over and toward the center. Repeat with the three remaining sides. Now the dough is ready for second fermentation.

Prepare four clean, dry quart containers with lids. Put 1 tablespoon olive oil in each quart container, swirling them to coat the sides with oil.

Spray nonstick cooking spray on a clean work surface, remove the dough from the bowl and place on the greased area. Cut the dough into 4 equal pieces—I like to use a scale for this part. If the dough is very sticky, you can oil your hands before you touch it.

For each piece of dough, pull the cut edges together, then turn it over to make a smooth ball. Gently place each ball in an oiled container and cover with the lid. Leave on the counter until they double or triple in size, two hours or more, depending on the starter's strength and the temperature of the room.

If you're not making the pizza immediately, you can slow the fermentation by placing the containers in the refrigerator for up to 5 days. A few hours before you plan to make the pizza, remove them from the refrigerator and let them come to room temperature on the counter, until they double or triple in size. This could take 2 hours or more. You can place it somewhere warm, like in the oven without the heat on, to speed up rising.

Preheat the oven to 500°F (remove the dough first if you've put it in the oven). Dust four quarter-size or two half-size baking sheets generously with semolina. If you have a pizza stone, put it in the bottom of the oven.

Remove a ball of dough from the container; the dough should be elastic. Gently stretch it by hand and place it in a prepared pan. If using a quarter-size baking sheet, stretch to fit the pan, leaving a ½ to 1-inch space around the border. If using a half-size baking sheet, stretch to fit about half of the pan, leaving space for a second pizza. Repeat with the remaining dough.

Now the pizzas are ready for the toppings. Smear ¼ cup of the tomato sauce on each pizza using the back of a spoon. Divide the toppings evenly among the pizzas, arranging the bamboo shoots, scallions, and mozzarella as you like (you will add the chrysanthemum greens later). Sprinkle with some salt.

Bake for 6 minutes, then take out the pizza, arrange the greens on top, and continue baking until the crust is golden brown and the cheese is bubbling, 2 to 6 minutes longer. Serve immediately.

HANAMI

Like most Japanese people, I love sakura, a blossoming cherry tree and the national tree of Japan. The delicate pink blossoms signify the first sign of spring. When the petals fall, they look like snowflakes—it's a very transitional time of the year. During the blossoming of the trees we look forward to embracing the warm weather, but also reflect on the changing season and the end of winter. There are a lot of hellos and good-byes in the season of sakura. The school year ends in March and the new one starts in April. People naturally gather around the cherry blossom trees and often bring food and drinks to have picnics. It's called hanami, or "flower viewing."

Sometimes you have to show up early to hold a spot under a good cherry tree. If you're looking to do hanami with a group of people, someone is designated to bring a blanket and wait. Someone else will bring bentos, and others will be responsible for beverages. Then, let the party start.

I took the tradition of hanami with me when I moved to New York. There is a significant number of sakura trees in the parks and streets of the city. As soon as it's warm enough to spend time outside after a long winter, I try to find a good place to picnic. When I was in my twenties, I used to go to Central Park with my Japanese friends, and we'd sit on our blankets and have a meal under the cherry trees. Later, after meeting Aaron, we would go to the New York Botanical Garden and do the same.

Now that we are so busy with kids and a restaurant, we are grateful to find any day during cherry blossom season when we can relax. Due to the rainy weather in the spring, we sometimes miss out on the sakura, but sometimes we get lucky. Picnicking in parks saved our sanity during the lockdown period of the pandemic. It was necessary for us to be out in nature and center ourselves.

Being able to sit down under a blossoming tree with friends and family, to slow down and to enjoy the day is so magical. We eat and bask in the soft spring light, deeply inhaling the warm air and welcoming the new growth. Our choice of picnic foods are usually a nice sando, cheese and charcuterie, or onigiri and tamagoyaki in a bento box. Whatever it is we're eating, it feels great to be out together in the sunshine. —Sawa

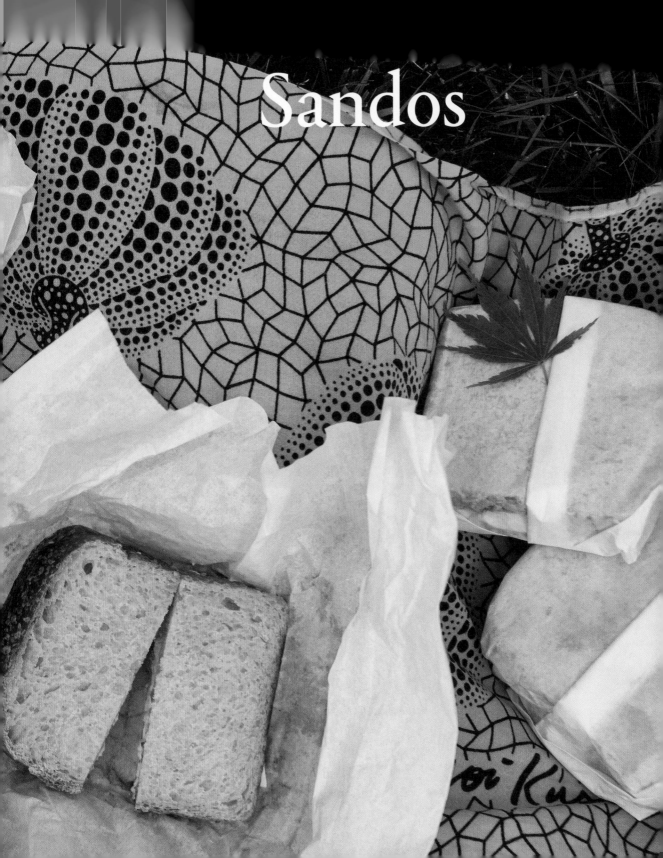

Sandos

サンド

A sandwich, or sando as it's called in Japan, is a simple thing. But the care you put into the ingredients and how you construct it can elevate it to new heights. A good sando starts with shokupan, a pillowy Japanese milk bread that, in our opinion, is the best sandwich bread there is. When we build a sando, we like to match the size of the fillings to the bread and place them in an even layer so when you start eating, the interior doesn't ooze out the sides. Some people like a messy sando, but we like to ensure that the first bite has as much filling as the last.

In Japan, there is no sando without shokupan, also known as Japanese milk bread. It's fluffy and soft, yet sturdy enough to handle serious fillings. Shokupan is the foundation for countless creations, such as mayonnaise-y tuna, tamago (egg salad), and crispy katsu (fried breaded pork cutlets). That's why it's the starting point for our chapter on sandos—they wouldn't be complete without it.

MAKES ONE 16-BY-4-INCH 2-POUND LOAF (ENOUGH FOR 10 TO 12 SANDWICHES) • ACTIVE TIME: 30 MINUTES • TOTAL TIME: 3 HOURS

In a small saucepan, scald the milk over high heat, heating just until bubbles form around the edges of the pan, then immediately remove from the heat. Pour in the water and set aside to cool to room temperature.

In the bowl of a stand mixer fitted with the dough hook attachment, mix the flour, sugar, salt, and yeast on low speed until incorporated. Increase the speed to medium, slowly pour in the milk and water mixture, and mix for 5 minutes, until the dough comes together in a sticky mass. Remove from the machine and poke the dough using your finger. If it feels wet and tacky, add another tablespoon of flour. Mix for 5 minutes on low speed, then poke the dough again. When it's ready, it should no longer stick to your finger. If it's still wet, add a tablespoon of flour and mix for a few more minutes on low speed, until the dough is smooth to the touch.

Add the butter and mix on low speed for 5 minutes, until the butter is incorporated and the dough is springy and does not stick to your fingers.

Coat a bowl with nonstick cooking spray. Form the dough into a ball and place in the bowl. Spray the top with nonstick cooking spray, cover with plastic wrap, and let the dough proof at room temperature until it has doubled in size, about an hour.

Coat the inside of a 16 × 4-inch Pullman loaf pan with cooking spray. Remove the dough from the bowl and place on a clean work surface. Gently punch the dough to get the air out. Using a bowl scraper or a knife, cut into four equal pieces and form each into a ball. Gently line them up side by side in the loaf pan. If the dough looks dry, spray with water to cover in a fine mist, or sprinkle lightly with wet fingertips. Cover with plastic wrap and let proof at room temperature until it is just about to touch the top of the plastic wrap, 1 to 2 hours.

Shokupan

Japanese Milk Bread

食パン

240g (1 cup) whole milk, plus more for brushing
230g (1 cup) water
780g (5¼ cups) bread flour, sifted, plus more as needed
50g (¼ cup) sugar
15g (5 teaspoons) kosher salt
8g (2½ teaspoons) active dry yeast
42g (3 tablespoons) unsalted butter, at room temperature
Cooking spray
4 or 5 ice cubes

continued

Variation:

DELI RYE SHOKUPAN:
For a shokupan reminiscent of Jewish rye, add 6g (2 teaspoons) toasted caraway seeds with the dry ingredients.

Preheat the oven to 400°F.

Remove the plastic wrap. Let the dough proof another 5 to 10 minutes until it crests over the edge of the loaf pan by about a ½ inch. Gently brush the top of the dough with a light coating of milk. Put the loaf in the oven, then throw 4 or 5 ice cubes onto the oven floor. (You can also put the ice cubes on a baking sheet and set on the oven floor.) If you don't have ice cubes, generously spray water into the oven immediately after you place the pan on the rack. (Both create steam, which helps the bread rise.)

Bake for 18 minutes. Rotate the loaf, and bake for another 18 minutes, until it has a nice brown crust. Remove the pan from the oven. Hold onto the sides firmly, then tip onto a cooling rack and let the loaf slide out. Place the loaf upright and let cool completely. Store in a plastic bag on your counter for a day, then refrigerate for 4 to 5 days, or slice and freeze in an airtight bag for up to a month.

Note Our sando recipes call for toasting sliced bread on one side, so the inner-facing side is crisp, and the outside remains pillowy. We spritz the bread with a little water and lightly toast it in a skillet with olive oil or butter. If eaten immediately, the toasted side brings texture to each bite. If packing for later, it acts as a barrier against the filling, keeping the bread firmer for longer.

I bake a loaf of Rakkenji Shokupan (page 102) every week using a Rakkenji starter, a naturally fermented leavening made from carrots, apples, Japanese mountain yam, and rice. The recipe was developed by a monk named Yugen Yamanouchi in Nara, Japan, as a wholesome alternative to conventional breads. To procure sourdough starter for this recipe, ask a local bakery or friends who bake—they may be happy to share. I've also had success using a pinch of active dry yeast to kick off the starter. If you can't get the mountain yam, Yukon Gold and russet potatoes work too. I try to get organic vegetables and do not peel the skin. Instead, I scrub them with a tawashi (page 30).

Unlike sourdough starter, you don't need to discard the Rakkenji starter to feed it (see Feeding and Maintaining a Starter, page 101). Even two weeks after it ripens, it still has the strength to ferment the dough. You can use the Rakkenji starter for so many things, like our Japanese Garden Pizza (page 89). If you bake with it regularly, the time invested pays off. **—Sawa**

Rakkenji Starter

楽健寺酵母

Boiling water

100g (3½ ounces) apple (any kind will do), unpeeled, washed, and cut into small chunks (about ½ cup)

100g (3½ ounces) carrot, unpeeled, scrubbed, and grated (about ½ cup)

70g (2½ ounces) Japanese mountain yam (nagaimo) or potato, such as russet or Yukon Gold, unpeeled, scrubbed, and cut into small chunks (about ⅓ cup)

80g (½ cup) cooked rice (white, brown, or multigrain will all work)

40g (3 tablespoons plus ½ teaspoon) sugar, preferably raw or unrefined

1g sea salt or a very small pinch

100g (about ½ cup) sourdough or Rakkenji starter or 1g (½ teaspoon) active dry yeast

70g to 175g (½ to 1¼ cups) bread flour

Fill a 2-quart glass jar with a lid all the way to the top with boiling-hot water and let sit for a few minutes to sterilize it. Pour out the water and let the jar air-dry.

In a blender or a food processor, combine the apple, carrot, mountain yam, rice, sugar, and salt. Start on low speed and gradually turn up to high and blend until you have a smooth puree. If the blender has trouble pureeing, add water, one tablespoon at a time, just enough to get things moving.

Pour into a large bowl. Add the sourdough starter and 70g (½ cup) of flour to start, and mix using a rubber spatula until fully incorporated. You want the consistency to be like a thick cake batter (❶, page 101). If it's too thin, add more flour as necessary, about 35g (¼ cup) at a time.

Transfer the mixture to the sterilized jar. Place the lid on, leaving it cracked open so the starter can breathe. Slide a rubber band down the container to the level of the starter in the jar (❷, page 101). Leave on your kitchen counter. Let the starter rise until it doubles in height (❸, page 101). The colder the temperature, the longer it will take to rise; it should take 6 to 8 hours, or up to 24 hours if you are making the starter for the first time. Be patient!

Once it has doubled, it will reach a point where it will start to collapse and sink back to the level where it started (where the rubber band is). Smell the starter. You should smell a bit of alcohol and a sweet, sour, and fruity aroma. Now your starter is ripe, and you are ready to make the dough. If you're not baking immediately, cover with the lid slightly ajar and refrigerate for up to 2 weeks.

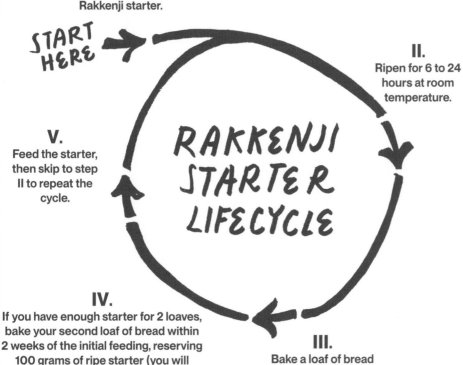

I.
Use sourdough starter or active dry yeast to make your first batch of Rakkenji starter.

START HERE →

II.
Ripen for 6 to 24 hours at room temperature.

V.
Feed the starter, then skip to step II to repeat the cycle.

RAKKENJI STARTER LIFECYCLE

IV.
If you have enough starter for 2 loaves, bake your second loaf of bread within 2 weeks of the initial feeding, reserving 100 grams of ripe starter (you will need this to feed your starter, and start the cycle over again).

III.
Bake a loaf of bread and refrigerate any excess starter.

FEEDING AND MAINTAINING A STARTER
Say you've used some of the ripe starter to make the dough, but you have leftovers. To keep it alive, you need to "feed" it. That means saving 100g of leftover ripe starter to make a fresh batch of the starter recipe. If you have less than 100g, the starter recipe will still work. I've made it with as little as 60g.

If the starter has been sitting for longer than 2 weeks (up to 2 months) and the top starts to turn gray, you can scrape off the top and discard. The remaining starter might not be good for baking, but it isn't dead yet. Just "feed" it again by using the old starter in a fresh batch of the starter recipe. It's surprisingly resilient. If you put care into it, you can keep it alive for a lifetime.

Rakkenji Shokupan

Rakkenji-Starter Milk Bread

楽健寺酵母の食パン

200g (¾ cup plus
   1 tablespoon) whole milk,
   plus more for brushing
200g (¾ cup plus
   2 tablespoons) water
215g (about 1 cup) ripe
   Rakkenji Starter (page 99)
35g (2 tablespoons plus
   2¼ teaspoons) sugar,
   preferably raw or
   unrefined
780g (5¼ cups) bread flour,
   plus more as needed
13g (2¼ teaspoons) fine
   sea salt or 5 teaspoons
   kosher salt
42g (3 tablespoons)
   unsalted butter, at room
   temperature and very soft
Neutral cooking oil,
   such as canola or
   vegetable, for greasing
   (or cooking spray)
4 or 5 ice cubes

The recipe for this naturally leavened milk bread was inspired by a monk named Yugen Yamanouchi, who owned a bakery with his wife in Nara, Japan, where they sold bread made from his Rakkenji starter (page 99). Though I didn't have the opportunity to try his bread before he retired, once I found out about it, I ordered his book from Japan and started experimenting. When I decided to include this special bread in our book, I emailed Yamanouchi and he gave me his blessing.

Working with a natural starter requires practice, and sometimes failure. A few times early on, I ended up with sad, flat, dense bread. But the success that came after was so rewarding: a bread that is deeply flavorful, sturdy yet easy to chew, with a lovely texture that develops from the gentle rise of natural yeast. Once I got the hang of it, the loaves quickly replaced store-bought bread in our home. **—Sawa**

**MAKES ONE 16 × 4-INCH 2-POUND LOAF (ENOUGH FOR 10 TO 12 SANDWICHES) •
ACTIVE TIME: 1 TO 1½ HOURS, DEPENDING ON IF YOUR STARTER IS RIPE •
TOTAL TIME: 1 TO 2 DAYS**

In a small saucepan, scald the milk over high heat, heating until bubbles form around the edges of the pan, then immediately remove from the heat. Pour in the water and set aside to cool to room temperature.

In the bowl of a stand mixer, combine the Rakkenji starter, sugar, and milk-water mixture and give it a couple of stirs until just incorporated.

Sift in the flour and salt. Using the dough hook attachment, mix on low speed for 5 minutes. Remove the bowl from the machine and poke the dough using your index finger. If the dough feels wet, add a tablespoon of bread flour. Continue mixing for another 5 minutes on low speed, then turn off the machine and poke the dough again. When the dough is ready, it should no longer stick to your finger.

Add the butter and mix for another minute on low speed, until fully incorporated. Remove the bowl from the mixer. Using damp hands or a rubber spatula, scrape the dough from the hook and the sides of the bowl.

Stretch and fold the dough: Form the dough into a single mass, set in a bowl, then perform a set of stretches and folds. To do this, wet your hands so the dough doesn't stick to them, pull up the side of the dough closest to you, stretch it up, and fold it over to the opposite side of the bowl, like you're making an envelope (❶ and ❷). Give the bowl a quarter-turn and repeat the stretching and folding. Keep rotating the bowl a quarter-turn until you have stretched the dough like this four times, once in each direction, and the bowl is back in its original position.

continued

Shape the dough into a ball: Turn the dough over in the bowl so that the top is smooth (❸ and ❹, page 103). Cover the bowl with a lid or plastic wrap so the dough doesn't dry out. Let rest at room temperature for 40 minutes.

Uncover the bowl, and repeat the stretch and folding. Cover the bowl again and let the dough rise for about 40 minutes. Repeat the stretching and folding again. Cover the dough and let rise for another 40 minutes. (In total, you will do four sets of stretches and folds over the course of 2 hours, after which it should have doubled in size.)

Remove the dough from the bowl and place it on a clean work surface. Gently punch the dough to get the air out. Using a plastic bowl scraper or a knife, cut into 4 equal portions and form each into a ball (I like to weigh them on a kitchen scale). Cover with a kitchen towel and let rest on the counter for 10 minutes.

Mist the inside of a 16 × 4-inch Pullman loaf pan with cooking spray. Uncover the dough balls and gently line them up in the pan (❺, page 103). If the dough looks dry, spray with water, just to cover in a fine mist. Cover with plastic wrap and let the dough proof at room temperature for 1 to 2 hours, until it just touches the top of the plastic. Remove the plastic and let the dough proof another 5 to 10 minutes, until it crests over the edge of the loaf pan by about ½ inch (❻, page 103). Alternately, once the loaf is formed, cover with plastic and let sit overnight in the refrigerator. It will proof slowly, but not fully. Remove from the refrigerator the next day and proceed with proofing. It can take 2 to 4 hours, depending on the temperature of the room.

Preheat the oven to 400°F.

Gently brush the top of the dough with a light coating of milk. Put the loaf in the oven, then throw 4 or 5 ice cubes onto the oven floor or generously spray water into the oven. (Both ice and water create steam, which helps the bread rise.)

Bake until it has a nice brown crust and the kitchen is filled with the aroma of freshly baked bread, about 36 minutes, rotating the loaf front to back halfway through. Remove the pan from the oven. Hold onto the sides firmly, then tip onto a cooling rack and let the loaf slide out. Place the loaf upright and let cool. Once cooled, store in a plastic bag, where it should keep 4 to 5 days without refrigeration, or slice and store in an airtight bag in the freezer for up to 1 month.

Veggie Deluxe Sando

with Shiso Pesto

夏野菜のデラックスサンド

1 large red bell pepper
3 tablespoons olive oil, plus
    1 teaspoon if roasting
    the pepper in the oven
1 zucchini, cut into slices
    ½ inch thick
Kosher salt and freshly
    ground black pepper
1 Japanese eggplant, cut on
    the diagonal into slices
    ½ inch thick
8 slices Shokupan (page 97),
    Rakkenji Shokupan
    (page 102), or your
    favorite sandwich bread,
    toasted on one side
¼ cup Shiso Pesto (page 36)
    or pesto of your choosing
¼ cup Kewpie mayonnaise or
    Chile Mayo (page 34)
8 slices provolone
Four ¼-inch-thick slices
    heirloom tomato
    (preferably as large as
    the sandwich bread)

This sandwich is a celebration of summer's bounty. We love the medley of seasonal vegetables—meaty sautéed zucchini and eggplant, sweet roasted peppers, juicy tomatoes—and shiso pesto adds an aromatic zing that enhances them all. If you don't have time to make or buy pesto, you can put fresh herbs on the sandwich and rub a clove of garlic on the bread instead. It won't be the same, but it will still be incredibly delicious.

SERVES 4 • TOTAL TIME: 30 TO 35 MINUTES

Turn on a gas burner to medium-high. Using heat-resistant tongs, roast the pepper over the flame until blackened all over, about 2 minutes per side. If you don't have a gas range, preheat the oven to 400°F and line a baking sheet with foil. Split the pepper down the middle, remove the seeds, and coat with a little olive oil. Place cut-side down on the prepared baking sheet and roast until the skin starts to blister, 15 to 20 minutes.

Place the roasted pepper in a plastic container with a lid. Cover and let sit for 15 minutes. Uncover, peel the skin, discard any seeds and stem, cut into 4 equal pieces, and set aside.

In a large skillet, heat 1 tablespoon of the olive oil over high heat. Lay the zucchini in the pan. Season with salt and pepper and cook until golden brown, about 2 minutes. Flip, season the other side, and cook until lightly browned and just cooked through, 1 to 2 minutes. Transfer to a plate to cool.

Wipe the pan clean with a paper towel. Heat the remaining 2 tablespoons olive oil over high heat. Lay the eggplant in the pan, season with salt and pepper, and cook until golden brown, 2 to 3 minutes. Flip, season the other side, and cook until soft and lightly browned, 1 to 2 minutes. Transfer to the plate with the zucchini to cool.

Arrange the bread toasted-side up. Spread 1 tablespoon pesto evenly over 4 slices. Spread 1 tablespoon Kewpie mayonnaise over the other 4 slices.

Place 2 slices of cheese over the bread with the mayonnaise. Layer the zucchini over the cheese, then top with eggplant, tomato, and a piece of roasted pepper, dividing them evenly among the sandos. Season with salt and black pepper. Top with the bread slices, pesto-side down, cut each sando in half, and serve.

Tamago Sando

Egg Salad Sandwich

卵サンド

8 eggs
⅔ cup Kewpie mayonnaise
¼ cup finely diced onion
½ teaspoon rice vinegar
Pinch of salt
Freshly ground black pepper
8 slices Shokupan (page 97),
    Rakkenji Shokupan
    (page 102), or your
    favorite sandwich bread,
    toasted on one side

Though most of the time that we spend in Japan we're being fed by Sawa's parents, one of our guilty pleasures is the egg salad sandwich from the Lawson konbini (convenience store). It's good enough to change your mind about what an egg salad sandwich can be. The key to this recipe (pictured on page 94) is high-quality eggs, plus Kewpie mayonnaise, which makes the salad extra creamy and savory. Diced onion adds subtle texture to each bite, and the black pepper makes your tongue tingle just a bit. When you're making something this simple, every ingredient counts, so splurge on the best eggs you can find. **—Aaron**

MAKES 4 SANDOS · TOTAL TIME: 20 MINUTES

Bring a small pot of water to boil over high heat. Add the eggs and let the water come back to a boil. Reduce the heat to medium and cook for 9 minutes. The eggs will be just shy of hard-boiled. Drain, then run under cold water to stop from cooking further.

Once cool enough to handle, peel the eggs, then finely chop. Place in a bowl with the mayonnaise, onion, vinegar, salt, and pepper and mix to combine.

Lay 4 slices of bread on a cutting board, toasted-side up. Divide the egg salad evenly among them, about ½ cup each, and spread in an even layer. Top with another slice of bread, toasted-side down. Cut in half crosswise and serve.

BENTO BOXES

Many of our recipes make for leftovers that are ideal for packing a bento box, the Japanese version of a lunch box, usually organized into small compartments that can fit a variety of foods. Bentos are everywhere in Japan, from konbini (convenience stores) to train stations, which often feature a dizzying array of elaborate bento that reflect a region's specialties.

When assembling a bento we like to get in as many food groups as possible for a balanced meal, and we pack things that can survive a few hours outside of the refrigerator. First, we'll decide on the starch. If going the bread route, a bento can be as simple as a few sandos and some pickles on the side. If choosing rice, onigiri or rice with some kind of protein are good options. Leftover Karaage (page 188) or Hambagu (page 200) work great, and Tamagoyaki (page 42) is a staple that pairs well with everything. Then, we round it out with as many vegetables as we can. Here are some of our favorite combinations, but the point of bento is to work with what you have to mix and match a perfect meal away from home.

Clockwise from top left, pictured on pages 110–111:

1. Onigiri stuffed with umeboshi and wrapped in nori, and furikake onigiri

2. Hambagu, karaage (Japanese fried chicken), gomaae broccoli (broccoli with sesame sauce)

3. Tamagoyaki (dashi rolled omelet), hijiki-ni (braised seaweed), tonkatsu (fried pork cutlet)

4. Hijiki-carrot rice

5. Harumaki (spring rolls), kinpira (braised burdock and carrots), tamagoyaki

6. Multigrain onigiri stuffed with shiozake (salted salmon)

7. Tamago (egg salad) and chicken katsu (fried chicken cutlet) sandos

8. Multigrain rice, shiozake, takuan (pickled daikon)

9. Tsukune (chicken meatballs), spinach ohitashi (spinach with soy sauce and bonito flakes), tamagoyaki

BTS

Bacon, Tomato, and Shiso

BTSサンド

8 slices thick-cut bacon
8 slices Shokupan (page 97),
    Rakkenji Shokupan
    (page 102), or your
    favorite sandwich bread,
    toasted on one side
½ cup Kewpie mayonnaise
1 very large heirloom tomato,
    roughly the size of the
    slice of bread, cut into
    4 slices ¾ inch thick
Kosher or flaky salt
    and freshly ground
    black pepper
12 shiso leaves
4 lettuce leaves, such as
    green leaf or romaine

In the summer, the shiso plants in our garden grow leaves the size of our hand. It only seemed natural to add them to another great summer delicacy, the BLT. The shiso delivers a beautiful floral flavor. It doesn't hurt that the herb is at its best right when tomatoes are reaching their peak. When we're shopping at the farmers' market, we look for heirloom tomatoes that are so big that just one slice can cover an entire piece of bread. Smaller tomatoes work, too—just remember to cut them thick.

SERVES 4 · TOTAL TIME: 15 MINUTES

In a large skillet, fry the bacon over medium heat until browned but not fully crispy, 4 to 6 minutes on each side. If you like your bacon crispier, fry it for an extra minute or two. Transfer the bacon to a plate lined with paper towels.

Lay the bread on a cutting board, toasted-side up, and spread 1 tablespoon of mayonnaise onto each slice. Place 2 slices of bacon onto each of 4 pieces of bread, top each with a tomato slice, and season with salt and pepper. Top each tomato with 3 shiso leaves and a lettuce leaf. Top with a slice of bread, mayo-side down. Cut each sandwich in half and serve.

Katsu in Japan refers to any cutlet that is breaded with panko crumbs and fried up nice and crispy. In this case, it's a chicken cutlet, sandwiched between two pieces of fluffy shokupan with Kewpie mayonnaise, okonomi sauce, and a healthy heap of cabbage slaw. It's a great sando to pack for the road, and it works just as well with leftover fried pork cutlet (Tonkatsu, page 193). If you're not familiar with panko bread crumbs, try this recipe and see why we love it so much for breading cutlets. It's a perfect crumb, coarse yet light, lending the fried exterior extra crunch without being even remotely heavy.

MAKES 4 SANDOS • TOTAL TIME: 1 HOUR

In a bowl, toss together the cabbage, carrot, sesame oil, vinegar, sugar, and 1 teaspoon of the salt. Let sit for at least 15 minutes or up to overnight to meld the flavors and soften the cabbage.

Place the chicken breasts in one layer on a baking sheet. Sprinkle the remaining 1 teaspoon salt evenly on both sides. Put the flour in a fine-mesh sieve and dust both sides of each breast with an even coating of flour. Shake off any excess.

Crack the eggs into a shallow dish large enough to hold a chicken breast, and beat using a fork. Put the panko into a similar-size dish. Prepare a large dish for the uncooked breaded cutlets. Line a large plate with a paper towel or fit a baking sheet with a cooling rack for the fried cutlets.

Dip each breast into the egg, coating both sides evenly, then transfer to the dish with the panko. Cover each side with panko and shake off any excess. Lay the breaded cutlet on the prepared dish and repeat with the remaining cutlets. Discard any extra egg or panko.

In a large cast-iron skillet or heavy-duty sauté pan, heat ¼ inch canola oil over medium heat. Drop a piece or two of panko into the pan to test the oil. If it sizzles immediately, it's time to fry the cutlets. Gently lay two into the pan and cook until the bottoms and sides are golden brown, 4 to 5 minutes. Using a pair of tongs or cooking chopsticks, gently flip and fry until the other side is golden brown and crispy, 4 to 5 minutes. Transfer to the towel-lined plate or cooling rack and sprinkle with more salt. Repeat with the remaining cutlets.

Lay the bread slices on a work surface, toasted-side up. Spread 1 tablespoon of mayonnaise onto each of 4 slices. Spread 1 tablespoon of okonomi sauce onto the other 4 slices. Put a chicken cutlet onto the slices with the mayo. Top with equal amounts of the cabbage slaw and the remaining slices of bread. Cut in half and serve with a pickle spear on the side.

Chicken Katsu Sando

Fried Chicken Cutlet Sandwich

チキンカツサンド

4 cups packed finely shredded green cabbage (¼ to ½ head, depending on the size)
½ cup finely shredded carrot (shredded on the medium holes of a box grater)
1 teaspoon toasted sesame oil
1 teaspoon rice vinegar
½ teaspoon sugar
2 teaspoons kosher salt, plus more for sprinkling
4 boneless, skinless chicken breasts (about 6 ounces each), pounded to a ½-inch thickness
¼ cup all-purpose flour
2 eggs
1½ cups panko bread crumbs
Canola oil or vegetable oil, for frying
8 slices Shokupan (page 97), Rakkenji Shokupan (page 102), or your favorite sandwich bread, toasted on one side
¼ cup Kewpie mayonnaise or Chile Mayo (page 34)
¼ cup okonomi sauce, homemade (page 34) or store-bought (we like Otafuku brand)
4 pickle spears

Hambagu Melt

ハンバーグホットサンド

4 tablespoons unsalted
    butter
1 yellow onion, thinly sliced
1 teaspoon kosher salt
Freshly ground black pepper
¼ cup Kewpie mayonnaise
2 tablespoons ketchup
1½ tablespoons small-diced
    pickles
8 slices Shokupan (page 97),
    Rakkenji Shokupan
    (page 102), or your
    favorite sandwich bread,
    such as rye or whole
    wheat
4 cooked Hambagu patties
    (page 200), halved
    horizontally, like a bagel
4 slices Swiss or Jarlsberg
    cheese
4 pickle spears

Our Japanese riff on the classic American patty melt relies on leftover meatloaf-like Hambagu (page 200), and Shokupan (page 97) in place of traditional rye bread. Since our son loves ketchup with the hambagu and we love Kewpie mayonnaise on sandwiches, we combine the two here, along with diced pickles, in what we believe to be the best Russian dressing.

MAKES 4 SANDOS • TOTAL TIME: 30 MINUTES IF USING LEFTOVER HAMBAGU; 1 HOUR 45 MINUTES IF MAKING THE HAMBAGU

Heat a small skillet over medium heat. Add 1 tablespoon of the butter, the onion, salt, and a few cracks of black pepper. Stir every 30 seconds or so until the onions are translucent, cooked through, and have started to brown and caramelize, 10 to 15 minutes. Remove from the heat and set aside.

In a small bowl, stir together the mayonnaise, ketchup, and diced pickles. Set the Russian dressing aside.

Lay 4 slices of bread out on a work surface. Spread 1 tablespoon of the Russian dressing on each slice. Place 2 halves of the hambagu patty onto 4 of the slices to cover the surface of the bread. Top the hambagu with a slice of cheese. Divide the cooked onions evenly among the sandwiches.

In a large skillet, melt 1 tablespoon of the butter over medium heat. Take the remaining bread and press into the melted butter, one piece at a time, coating one side evenly with butter. Smear 1 tablespoon of Russian dressing onto the unbuttered side of each slice, then place on the sandwich, dressing-side down.

Melt another 1 tablespoon of the butter in the pan and reduce the heat to medium-low. Place 2 of the sandos in the pan, buttered-side up. Place a lid that is slightly smaller than the pan directly onto the sandwiches to apply gentle pressure as they cook. If you don't have a lid, simply press gently with a spatula. Cook, rotating in the pan once or twice to get even color, until the bread is golden brown, about 5 minutes. Flip and repeat on the other side. When both sides are golden brown and the cheese has melted, transfer to a cutting board. Repeat with the remaining two sandwiches and remaining 1 tablespoon butter.

Slice each sandwich in half crosswise, plate with a pickle spear, and serve.

Noodles

麺類

Japan is a country obsessed with noodles. Any place you go has its own specialty. From chewy Sanuki udon hand-crafted in Kagawa prefecture to mass-consumed ramen noodles, which are found everywhere in all styles—artisanal, instant, thick, thin, wavy, straight, in broth, without broth, and countless other variations. There are chilled noodles for the warm weather, and hot noodles for slurping in cooler months. Even Italian pasta has become a national favorite. No matter the origins, noodles are a comfort to us.

When it's cold out, I make udon in hot broth at least once a week. It's the perfect vehicle for warming your body. In its simplest form, this dish is called kake udon, which is just broth poured over noodles, *kake* meaning "poured." In Japan, a heartier version is called *sutamina* udon ("stamina" in Japanese), because it is loaded with energy-giving ingredients. I typically use shiitake, spinach, beef, and eggs, but I change things depending on what's in season and what I have on hand. This is a quick, everyday comfort food that I don't have to think too much about, and it never fails to satisfy. **—Sawa**

SERVES 4 • TOTAL TIME: 30 MINUTES

To make the broth: In a pot, combine the mirin and sake and bring to a boil over high heat. Boil until the alcohol cooks out, about 2 minutes. Add the dashi, salt, soy sauce, and sugar. Bring to a boil, stirring to dissolve the sugar. Taste and add more salt to taste. Remove from the heat and set aside.

To prepare the toppings: Bring a large pot of water with a lid to a boil over high heat. Set up a small bowl filled with ice water.

Gently lower the eggs into the boiling water. For a soft-boiled egg with a runny yolk, remove after 7 minutes and place in the ice bath. (Cover the pot and turn the heat down to low for cooking the noodles later.) When the eggs are cool enough to handle, peel and set aside.

In a large skillet, heat the canola oil over high heat. Add the shiitake and cook, stirring frequently, until they start to brown, 2 to 3 minutes. Add the beef and cook, stirring occasionally, until it's cooked halfway and there isn't much rosy color left, 1 to 2 minutes. Add the spinach, sake, sugar, and soy sauce. Cook until the meat is cooked through and the spinach is wilted, 2 to 3 minutes. Remove from the heat and set aside.

To assemble: Bring the pot of water back to a boil over high heat. Cook the udon noodles according to the package directions (see How to Cook Japanese Noodles, page 124). Drain and divide among four large soup bowls.

Bring the pot of broth back to a boil over high heat. Distribute evenly among the bowls. Divide the mushrooms, beef, and spinach among the bowls, then place an egg in each, along with some scallions. Serve immediately with shichimi togarashi for sprinkling.

Sutamina Udon

Udon in Hot Broth with Beef, Egg, and Vegetables

スタミナうどん

Broth
¼ cup mirin
2 tablespoons sake
4 cups Dashi (page 33) or 4 teaspoons dashi powder mixed into 4 cups water
2 teaspoons kosher salt, plus more to taste
2 tablespoons soy sauce
4 teaspoons sugar

Toppings
4 eggs
2 tablespoons canola oil or other neutral oil
8 shiitake mushrooms caps, thinly sliced
8 ounces beef (such as sirloin, rib eye, or chuck roll), cut into slices about ⅛ inch thick
1 bunch spinach, washed
2 tablespoons sake
1 teaspoon sugar
1 tablespoon soy sauce

Assembly
2 pounds frozen or 1 pound dried udon noodles (such as Inaniwa, Sanuki, or Sanuki-style)
2 scallions, thinly sliced
Shichimi togarashi (optional), for sprinkling

Chilled Udon with Tsuyu

冷やしうどん

2 pounds frozen or 1 pound dried udon noodles (such as Inaniwa, Sanuki, or Sanuki-style) or somen noodles
A few ice cubes
Tsuyu (recipe follows)
2 scallions, thinly sliced
1 tablespoon finely grated fresh ginger
1 or 2 (8 × 7-inch) sheets nori (optional), shredded or torn into confetti-like pieces
1 to 2 tablespoons toasted sesame seeds (optional), ground

Summer for us is all about chilled udon noodles. Unlike a hot broth, the dipping sauce is more concentrated, so it's meant for dunking the noodles in and then pulling them out with chopsticks, leaving a light coating on the outside to flavor them. This smoky-savory tsuyu (dashi-soy dipping sauce) is our go-to. We place garnishes on the table, like scallions, grated ginger, shredded nori, and ground toasted sesame seeds, so that everyone can flavor their individual bowls of tsuyu when they sit down to eat. It's a fun, interactive part of the meal. On a hot summer day, we put ice cubes on top of the noodles so they stay chilled and to keep them from sticking. If our kids want to add ice to their dipping sauce, we let them. Thin, quick-cooking somen noodles are another wonderful option for this dish.

SERVES 4 • TOTAL TIME: 15 MINUTES

Bring a large pot of water to a boil over high heat.

Drop the noodles into the boiling water, stir, and cook according to the package directions (see How to Cook Japanese Noodles, page 124). Drain in a colander, run under cold water until completely chilled, then drain again. Transfer to a serving bowl and place a few cubes of ice on top to keep the noodles cold.

Set the table with four small bowls (to be filled later with dipping sauce and garnishes). Place the scallions and grated ginger in small dishes on the table. If using the nori and sesame seeds, also put them in small dishes. Place the tsuyu dipping sauce and chilled noodles in the center of the table. To eat, spoon a few tablespoons of the tsuyu into your bowl and add a sprinkle of scallions, a small pinch of grated ginger, nori, and sesame seeds. Dip the noodles into the bowl of seasoned dipping sauce before each bite.

Tsuyu

Dashi-Soy Dipping Sauce

¼ cup sake
¼ cup mirin
1 tablespoon sugar
¼ cup soy sauce
1 cup Dashi (page 33) or 1 teaspoon dashi powder mixed into 1 cup water

MAKES 1¾ CUPS

In a small pot, combine the sake, mirin, and sugar and bring to a boil over medium-high heat. Boil until the alcohol cooks out, stirring once or twice to dissolve the sugar, about 2 minutes. Stir in the soy sauce and dashi, return to a boil, and remove from the heat. Transfer to a small jar with a lid. Let cool to room temperature and use right away, or cover and store in the refrigerator for up to 1 week.

HOW TO COOK JAPANESE NOODLES

When it comes to cooking Japanese noodles, there are a few basics to keep in mind: First, you don't need to season the water. Unlike Italian pasta, many of the noodles already have enough salt in them, or are served in sauces or broths that will season them sufficiently. After dropping the noodles into the boiling water, always give them a stir so they don't stick.

Cooking times for noodles can vary depending on whether they're dried, fresh, or frozen, and the desired texture depends on the type of noodle. Whenever you can, follow the cooking directions on the package. If you are unable to read them (often they're in Japanese), here are some guidelines to follow:

Malony ❶ A dried gluten-free glass noodle made from potato starch, malony has a light, chewy texture. It cooks in 4 to 5 minutes, but when eating it in hotpot, we like to parcook the malony for 2 minutes and finish cooking it at the table.

Ramen Fresh ramen noodles can take anywhere from 1 minute for the thinner variety ❷ to 3 minutes for thicker, wavy temomi ramen ❸. Regardless of the style, the texture should be firm and springy.

Soba ❹ Soba noodles come fresh, frozen, or dried, and cook quickly—1 to 2 minutes for fresh or frozen, 4 to 6 minutes for dried. They will be tender and possibly brittle, depending on how much buckwheat flour is used when making them. Dried soba noodles are often packed in 100-gram bundles; we consider one of these to be a single portion size.

Somen ❺ Thin somen noodles are dried and fast-cooking, generally requiring 1 to 2 minutes in boiling water. Cooked somen will be smooth, silky, and easy to slurp.

Udon Among the varieties of udon noodle, semi-dry Sanuki udon ❻ takes the longest to cook, 10 to 14 minutes, and should be sturdy and chewy when done. Frozen Sanuki-style udon ❼ will have the same texture, but the noodles are parcooked, and only require 2 to 3 minutes of boiling. Inaniwa udon ❽, a dried variety, cooks in 4 to 6 minutes, and will have a silky, smooth texture.

We call our interpretation of Vietnamese pho "faux" because it's our attempt at reproducing the complex, aromatic soup with the ingredients we usually have at home. Since we always have Japanese noodles, we substitute silky Inaniwa udon for the similarly textured rice noodles used in pho. If we don't have lemongrass or Vietnamese rock sugar, we use lemon zest and granulated sugar. We infuse the chicken stock and dashi with rich, beefy flavor by using oxtail. We never skip toasting the spices and getting a good char on the onion, which are both crucial to developing the flavor of the soup. Just like real pho, faux pho is full of contrasts: rich and light, braised and fresh. The results are not entirely authentic, but they are deeply satisfying.

SERVES 4 TO 6 • ACTIVE TIME: 30 MINUTES • TOTAL TIME: 3½ HOURS

In a small dry skillet, toast the fennel, peppercorns, coriander, star anise, cloves, and cinnamon over low heat until they start to smell aromatic, 3 to 4 minutes. Place the toasted spices, along with the lemon zest and ginger, in an empty tea sachet, or wrap in a cheesecloth or a coffee filter and tie them securely.

Set the onion halves directly over the open flame of a gas burner on medium-high heat. Char all over, rotating every few minutes. (Alternatively, place the onion halves on a pan and char under the broiler.)

In a 4-quart soup pot, combine the oxtail, chicken stock, and dashi and bring to a boil over high heat, skimming any foam or scum that rises to the surface. (This will make the soup clearer looking and cleaner tasting.) Reduce to a low simmer so that it's gently bubbling. Add the sachet of aromatics, charred onion, sugar, and fish sauce. Simmer, partially covered, until the oxtail is falling off the bone and the meat is very tender, about 3 hours. If the liquid has reduced, add enough water to maintain the level you started with. Remove from the heat, discard the sachet, and let the broth sit undisturbed for about 10 minutes. Using a ladle, skim off any fat (which will appear clear and shiny) that has risen to the surface. (Alternatively, refrigerate overnight, remove the fat from the surface once it has congealed, and reheat over high heat before serving.)

To assemble: Bring a large pot of water to a boil.

Cook the udon noodles according to the package directions (see How to Cook Japanese Noodles, page 124). Drain and divide evenly among four large soup bowls.

Divide the bean sprouts, cilantro, scallions, and sliced raw beef equally among the bowls and arrange them on top of the noodles. Ladle the hot broth and a piece of oxtail into each bowl. Serve immediately with lime wedges and with sriracha and hoisin sauce on the side, if desired.

Faux Pho

フェイク・フォー

Broth
1 teaspoon fennel seeds
1 teaspoon black peppercorns
1 teaspoon coriander seeds
1 star anise
2 whole cloves
1-inch piece of cinnamon stick
Strips of zest cut off 1 lemon with a vegetable peeler or a 5-inch piece lemongrass, bruised with the back of a knife to release the aroma
3-inch piece of fresh ginger, cut into thirds
1 yellow onion, halved lengthwise
2 pounds oxtail (cut into 2-inch pieces) or bone-in short-rib
6 cups chicken stock
6 cups Dashi (page 33) or 2 tablespoons dashi powder mixed into 6 cups water
1 tablespoon sugar or ½-ounce piece of rock sugar
¼ cup fish sauce

Assembly
2 (6.34-ounce/180g) packages of Inaniwa udon noodles
2 cups bean sprouts
1 bunch cilantro, stems and leaves, cut into 2-inch lengths
2 scallions, thinly sliced
4 ounces thinly sliced beef rib eye or sirloin (Buying and Slicing Meat, page 148)
1 lime, cut into 4 to 6 wedges
Sriracha and hoisin sauce (optional), for serving

Spaghetti Napolitan

Ketchup Pasta with Bacon and Onions

ナポリタン

Salt

1½ cups ½-inch diced bacon (6 to 8 slices)

1 large yellow onion, thinly sliced

1 red bell pepper, thinly sliced

⅓ cup sake

¾ cup ketchup

1½ tablespoons Worcestershire sauce

1 tablespoon soy sauce

½ cup water

12 ounces spaghetti

¾ cup grated Parmigiano-Reggiano cheese

Freshly cracked black pepper

Spaghetti Napolitan, known affectionately as ketchup pasta in our house, is a great example of yoshoku, a Western food that's been adopted by the Japanese, in this case creating something not authentically Italian nor Japanese, but all its own. I was skeptical at first—it took Sawa making her recipe to win me over. It's a quick weeknight dinner and great for kids. The ketchup, onions, and peppers add just a touch of sweetness that they really like. Round it out with smoky bacon, soy sauce, and Worcestershire, and you've got a modern classic. **—Aaron**

SERVES 4 • TOTAL TIME: 30 MINUTES

Bring a large pot of water to a boil over high heat and salt it to taste like the sea.

In a large sauté pan, cook the bacon over medium heat, stirring frequently, until it turns golden brown but not crispy and has released some fat, 7 to 8 minutes. Add the onion and bell pepper and cook, stirring occasionally, until the onion is translucent and the pepper is soft, 6 to 8 minutes. Add the sake and cook until the liquid has reduced by half, about 1 minute. Stir in the ketchup, Worcestershire sauce, soy sauce, and the ½ cup water. Remove from the heat and set aside.

When the pot of water has come to a boil, drop in the spaghetti and cook to al dente according to the package directions. Drain the spaghetti and add it to the sauté pan. Cook over medium heat and toss together until the noodles are coated, 3 to 4 minutes. Remove from the heat and toss in half of the grated Parmigiano-Reggiano. Stir until fully incorporated. Taste your pasta at this point, and add more salt, if needed. Crack in some freshly ground black pepper. Sprinkle with the remaining grated cheese and serve immediately.

Mentaiko spaghetti is pasta mixed with butter or mayo and mentaiko, also known as spicy cod roe. You'll find this dish at izakayas, but it's popular for home cooks, too. Aaron came up with this deluxe version for me, inspired by years of cooking seafood pasta at Italian restaurants. The real secret is cooking the noodles in the sauce to take on the briny flavor of the clams. You can get frozen mentaiko roe, or a tube of prepared mentaiko paste, at a Japanese grocery. If using frozen roe, thaw it first, then open the membrane and use the eggs inside. Both come in varying levels of heat (we like mild). Leftover mentaiko is great eaten over rice. —**Sawa**

SERVES 4 • TOTAL TIME: 45 MINUTES

Bring a large pot of water to a boil over high heat and salt it to taste like the sea.

In a large sauté pan with a lid, warm the olive oil and garlic over medium heat, swirling the pan until the garlic turns golden. Add the chile flakes, thyme, and bay leaf and swirl the pan a couple more times to release the aromas. Add the tomato and cook over high heat, stirring frequently until broken down and soft, about 4 minutes. Add the clams and wine and bring to a boil. Cover, reduce the heat to medium, and cook until the clams open, 5 to 7 minutes. Uncover and remove from the heat. You will have a lot of liquid in the pan, about 1½ cups, but that's good—the pasta will soak it up. Using tongs, transfer the clams to a bowl. (If you prefer, you can remove the clams from the shells.)

Drop the spaghetti into the boiling water and stir immediately. (You can start this step while the clams are cooking.) Cook about 2 minutes less than the package directions. Taste for doneness—you want it just shy of al dente (it will finish cooking in the sauce). Drain and transfer the spaghetti to the pan with the sauce.

Add the zucchini, shrimp, and squid and bring to a boil over high heat. Cook, stirring frequently so the pasta absorbs the sauce, until the shrimp and squid are cooked through and the zucchini is floppy but not too soft, 4 to 6 minutes. The sauce should look a bit creamy and cling to the pasta. Taste a noodle for doneness (we like it al dente). If the pan gets too dry before the spaghetti is finished cooking, add a few tablespoons of water at a time and continue cooking until the spaghetti is cooked to your liking. If there is too much liquid in the pan, let it cook without disturbing for a minute or two until the sauce has reduced and been absorbed more by the pasta.

Return the clams to the pan along with the mentaiko, butter, mitsuba, and lemon juice and remove from the heat. Toss the pasta just until the butter melts, the mentaiko is evenly distributed, and the pasta takes on a rosy color. Top with nori and serve immediately.

Mentaiko Seafood Spaghetti

海鮮明太子スパゲッティ

Salt
3 tablespoons olive oil
3 garlic cloves, thinly sliced
Pinch of chile flakes
1 sprig of thyme
1 bay leaf
1½ cups diced tomato (about 1 large tomato)
18 littleneck clams, soaked in salty water overnight in the refrigerator to purge of sand, and scrubbed clean
1½ cups white wine
12 ounces spaghetti
1 small zucchini, cut into ⅛-inch-wide ribbons 3 inches long (about 2 cups)
8 medium shrimp, peeled, deveined, and halved horizontally
8 ounces cleaned squid with tentacles, tubes sliced into ½-inch rings
3 tablespoons mentaiko roe or paste
2 tablespoons unsalted butter
3 tablespoons chopped mitsuba or parsley
2 tablespoons fresh lemon juice
A handful of shredded or torn nori

Cold Sesame Mazemen

豚と椎茸の胡麻まぜそば

Sesame Sauce

⅔ cup unsweetened plain
    soy milk
⅔ cup chilled Dashi (page 33)
    or 1 teaspoon of dashi powder
    mixed into ⅔ cup cold water
2 tablespoons plus 2 teaspoons
    soy sauce
2 tablespoons mirin
3 tablespoons plus 1 teaspoon
    tahini
1 tablespoon rice vinegar

Pork, Mushrooms, and Peppers

2 tablespoons toasted sesame oil
8 ounces thinly sliced boneless
    pork shoulder
8 large shiitake mushroom caps,
    thinly sliced
1 cup thinly sliced shishito,
    poblano, or bell pepper
2 tablespoons sake
2 tablespoons soy sauce
2 tablespoons mirin
2 tablespoons sugar

Assembly

1 pound fresh thick ramen
    noodles, preferably temomi
1 Japanese or Persian (mini)
    cucumber, or ½ English
    cucumber, thinly sliced
    (about 1 cup)
2 scallions, thinly sliced
1 tablespoon toasted sesame seeds
Chili oil (optional), for drizzling

Mazemen is a type of ramen served with sauce instead of broth. *Maze* means "mix," and *men* means "noodle," so when eating mazemen you're supposed to mix it well to incorporate all the ingredients. We love this dish because it reminds us of cold sesame noodles, but even better. Ramen is all about the relationship between the noodles and broth, or sauce in this case. The thicker or richer the broth or sauce is, the fatter the noodle should be, which is why we use chubby temomi ramen.

Any unsweetened and plain soy milk will work for this recipe, but if you live near an Asian grocery, pick up some fresh, high-quality soy milk, or a shelf-stable variety, such as Kikkoman.

SERVES 4 • TOTAL TIME: 45 MINUTES

Bring a large pot of water to a boil.

To make the sesame sauce: In a blender, combine the soy milk, dashi, soy sauce, mirin, tahini, and vinegar and blend until fully mixed, for just a few seconds. Transfer to a container with a lid and refrigerate. You can make the sesame sauce up to 3 days ahead.

To prepare the pork, mushrooms, and peppers: In a skillet, heat the sesame oil over high heat. When the oil is shimmering, add the pork shoulder and cook, stirring occasionally, until lightly browned, 2 to 3 minutes. Add the shiitake mushrooms and peppers and cook, stirring a few times, until lightly browned, about 2 minutes. Add the sake, soy sauce, mirin, and sugar and cook until the sauce is reduced by about half, 1 to 3 minutes. Transfer to a bowl and set aside.

To assemble: Prepare an ice bath by filling a large bowl that a colander can fit into with cold water and ice cubes.

Drop the noodles into the boiling water and stir immediately. Cook according to the package directions (see How to Cook Japanese Noodles, page 124). Drain the noodles in a colander, then immediately plunge the colander with the noodles into the ice bath to stop them from cooking. Once the noodles are fully chilled, drain thoroughly.

Divide the noodles among four serving bowls. Divide the sesame sauce and the pork, mushroom, and pepper mixture, along with its sauce, evenly among the bowls of noodles. Garnish with the cucumber, scallions, and toasted sesame seeds. Drizzle on chili oil if you like it spicy. Mix well before eating.

Note For a vegan version of this dish, leave out the pork and substitute vegetable stock for dashi.

This soup is a Jewish-Japanese hybrid that Sawa and I have fine-tuned over the years. To me, it makes perfect sense. With Jewish people spread throughout the world for so long, our food has always balanced tradition and local flavor. So why not put ramen noodles in a bowl of matzoh ball soup? I'd like to think the Jews of Japan would approve.

This is not the exact matzoh ball ramen that we serve at Shalom Japan, but it's the way we cook it at home. We start with a whole chicken and cut off the breasts first (see Note), so we can poach them and keep them moist. Kombu and ginger make their way into the broth, as do hand-shaped matzoh balls and a tangle of fresh ramen noodles. Using a whole bird usually leaves us with leftover chicken. We like to mix it with Kewpie mayonnaise and diced onion for a delicious chicken salad. **—Aaron**

SERVES 4 TO 6 • ACTIVE TIME: 1 HOUR • TOTAL TIME: 5 HOURS

To make the soup: Remove the breast meat from the chicken with the skin intact (see Note) and place on a plate. Season both sides with 1 teaspoon of the salt and refrigerate. Remove the chicken legs by dislocating the thigh bones at the joint where they meet the back. Slice along the joint to detach.

In a large stockpot with a lid, combine the chicken carcass and legs (but not the breasts) and the water. Bring to a boil over high heat, taking care to skim any foam or other impurities that rise to the surface. Reduce the heat to a low simmer. Add the kombu, bay leaf, ginger, and the remaining 3 tablespoons salt. Cover and cook until the meat is tender and comes off the bone easily, 1½ hours. Check periodically to be sure it's only gently simmering, adjusting the heat if necessary.

Meanwhile, to start the matzoh balls: In a small bowl, combine the matzoh meal, baking powder, and salt and thoroughly combine using a fork or your hands. Add the canola oil and combine well, making sure the fat is evenly distributed. In another small bowl, beat the eggs with the 1 teaspoon water. Pour the eggs into the matzoh meal mixture and mix well. Put a layer of plastic wrap directly on the surface of the matzoh ball batter and refrigerate for at least 30 minutes.

After the chicken has been simmering for 1½ hours, use tongs and a slotted spoon to carefully fish the chicken legs out of the stock. When they're cool enough to handle, pick the meat off the bones, put in a container, cover, and refrigerate until ready to use. Return the bones to the pot, cover, and continue to gently simmer for another 1½ hours.

continued

Home-Style Matzoh Ball Ramen

マッツォボールラーメン

Chicken Soup
1 whole chicken (4 pounds)
3 tablespoons plus 1 teaspoon kosher salt
4 quarts water
1 (6-inch) square of kombu
1 bay leaf
1-inch piece of fresh ginger

Matzoh Balls
½ cup matzoh meal
1½ teaspoons baking powder
¼ teaspoon kosher salt
2 tablespoons canola oil, melted duck fat, or melted chicken fat
2 eggs
1 teaspoon water

For Finishing
1 bunch fresh dill, rinsed
1 bunch curly parsley, rinsed
1 carrot, peeled and cut into 1-inch pieces
1 small parsnip, peeled and cut into 1-inch pieces
2 celery stalks, cut into 1-inch pieces
1 yellow onion, quartered
Kosher salt
1 pound fresh ramen noodles
2 scallions, thinly sliced
Chili oil (optional), such as S&B brand
4 to 6 (4 × 2-inch) pieces of nori, for garnish

To finish: Uncover the stock and add the dill and parsley. Add the breasts to the simmering stock, cover, and simmer until cooked through, 12 to 16 minutes. Carefully remove and check for doneness using a metal skewer or the tip of a knife inserted into the thickest part of the breast. If it's cooked, the skewer should be very warm to the touch. If it's not, poach for a few more minutes. Transfer the breasts to a plate to cool. Strain the stock through a sieve into another large pot. (Discard the bones and aromatics.)

Bring a large pot of water to a boil over high heat for the noodles.

Add the carrot, parsnip, celery and onion to the stock. Bring to a boil over high heat.

Remove the matzoh ball batter from the refrigerator. Wet your hands to prevent sticking, then roll 8 to 10 balls the size of large marbles (about 1 heaping tablespoon), squeezing once or twice to lightly compress. Drop in the boiling pot of soup. Cover, then reduce the heat to medium, with the soup at a rolling boil. Cook until the matzoh balls have about tripled in size, are soft on the outside and a little spongy in the center, about 30 minutes. Cut one open to test; if they're undercooked, the center will be dark and dense.

Add the leg meat to the soup to warm through. Season with salt, anywhere from 1 to 3 teaspoons. (The broth needs to be salty because the noodles will absorb the seasoning from the soup.) Thinly slice the chicken breasts and set aside.

Drop the ramen noodles into the boiling water and stir. Cook according to the package directions (see How to Cook Japanese Noodles, page 124). Drain and distribute among serving bowls.

Ladle the broth over the ramen in the bowls, along with some vegetables, the leg meat, and one or two matzoh balls. Lay a few slices of the breast into each bowl, sprinkle with the scallions and chili oil (if using), and stand a piece of nori along the edge. Serve immediately.

Note To remove the chicken breasts, place the chicken on a cutting board breast-side up, with the legs facing you. Starting at the breastbone, slice downward, running your knife along the bone, slightly left of the center of the breast. When you hit the rib cage, angle the knife away toward the left breast, and slice the meat off the bone, pulling the breast away from the rib cage with your free hand. Keep slicing and pulling until you have detached the breast meat. Repeat with the other breast.

This stir-fried noodle dish is wildly popular throughout Japan, and there are so many versions. It's sold in instant noodle form at konbini (convenience stores) and can be found cooked on a flattop griddle by street vendors for a quick meal on the go. When I was in high school, the school cafeteria sold yakisoba-pan, which is yakisoba on a hotdog bun. Weird, I know, but it was one of my go-to items for lunch when I needed stamina. In this recipe we don't call for the bun, but feel free to give it a try. At home, instead of traditional sliced pork, I use aburaage (fried tofu), and often add a sunny-side up egg on top because a runny yolk makes just about anything better. You can certainly use any meat and vegetables you like—it's a great recipe for fridge clean-outs.   **—Sawa**

SERVES 4 TO 6 • TOTAL TIME: 30 MINUTES

Bring a large pot of water to boil over high heat for the ramen noodles.

Meanwhile, in a large wok or a large (14-inch) sauté pan, heat the canola oil over high heat until it shimmers. Add the onion and cook, stirring occasionally, until it just starts to brown, 1 to 2 minutes. Add the cabbage, shiitake, bell pepper, garlic, and salt and continue cooking, stirring occasionally, until the vegetables are soft but not mushy, 4 to 5 minutes. Add the aburaage, stir a few more times, and remove from the heat. Stir in the okonomi sauce, soy sauce, and sesame oil and set aside.

If using eggs, fry them as you like them before boiling the ramen noodles. We prefer them sunny-side up.

Drop the ramen noodles into the boiling water, stir, and cook according to the package directions (see How to Cook Japanese Noodles, page 124). Drain the noodles well, then add to the pan with the cooked vegetables. Cook over medium heat, stirring thoroughly to incorporate the noodles and the vegetables, and to coat well with the sauce, about 3 minutes. Remove from the heat and divide among serving plates. Top with the sliced scallions, fried eggs, aonori, and bonito flakes. Serve immediately.

Yakisoba

Stir-Fried Ramen Noodles

焼きそば

2 tablespoons canola oil or
   other neutral oil
1 yellow onion, thinly sliced
2 cups shredded cabbage
6 to 8 shiitake mushroom
   caps, thinly sliced
1 green bell pepper,
   thinly sliced
2 garlic cloves, minced
1 teaspoon kosher salt
2 (3 × 6-inch) pieces
   aburaage, thinly sliced
1 cup okonomi sauce,
   homemade (page 34)
   or store-bought
2 teaspoons soy sauce
1 teaspoon toasted sesame oil
4 eggs (optional)
1 pound fresh ramen noodles
2 scallions, green part only,
   thinly sliced
1 teaspoon aonori (optional)
¼ cup bonito flakes
   (optional)

New Year's Eve Soba with Kakiage Tempura

年越しそばとかき揚げ

Eating soba on New Year's Eve is a Japanese tradition. There are many explanations for why, but one story goes that people started eating soba in the Edo era to symbolize "cutting" bad luck and hardships. Japanese people tend to be superstitious. Soba noodles, made with varying amounts of buckwheat flour, are low in gluten, and henceforth easier to "break" than noodles made from only wheat flour, such as udon or ramen.

Whatever the reason, I love the combination of noodles, tempura, and tsuyu (dashi-soy dipping sauce). You dunk the tempura so it can soak up the delicious sauce, or plunge the noodles in and slurp them out.

Kakiage is a type of tempura usually made from vegetables or seafood "mixed together" ("kakimazeru" in Japanese) and fried ("ageru"). Before you make the tempura batter, have the vegetables cut and ready to go, so the batter doesn't sit too long and become gummy. Feel free to come up with your own kakiage combinations; carrot, green beans, and burdock all are good options, as are baby shrimp and squid. **—Sawa**

Bring a large pot of water to a boil for the soba.

In a large bowl, mix the flour, cornstarch, and salt until well combined. Add the seltzer and ice cubes. Mix until just combined, taking care not to overmix, or else too much gluten will form and the pancakes will be gummy. It's okay if it's a little lumpy. The mixture should be the consistency of pancake batter. If it's too thick, add a splash of seltzer. Keep in mind that the ice will melt and the batter will thin out as it does. Add the onion, corn, bell pepper, and green peas and mix with the tempura batter until just combined.

Set the oven to its lowest possible temperature to keep the kakiage warm. Line a baking sheet with paper towels, or set a cooling rack in a sheet pan.

Pour about ½ inch of oil into a large, deep, cast-iron skillet, and heat over medium-high to about 350°F on a deep-fry thermometer, or until a drop of tempura batter sizzles and floats when dropped into the oil. Using a large spoon or measuring cup, scoop about ½ cup of the kakiage mixture into the oil and flatten it just a bit so you have a thick pancake. Add as many as you can fit in the pan without crowding or letting the fritters touch. Fry the kakiage until the edges and bottom are golden brown, 5 to 7 minutes. Using cooking chopsticks or a spatula, carefully flip, and cook until the other side is golden brown and crispy, 5 to 7 minutes longer. Remove a kakiage and check if it is done by cutting it open just a bit. The vegetables in the center should be cooked (the onions should be slightly translucent and the bell pepper soft). Transfer to the lined baking sheet or cooling rack and slide into the oven to keep warm until ready to serve. Repeat with the remaining batter (you should get 8 to 10 kakiage total).

Drop the soba noodles into the boiling water and cook according to the package directions (see How to Cook Japanese Noodles, page 124). Drain in a colander and rinse under cold running water to chill. Drain well and transfer to a large serving bowl.

Put the kakiage on a platter and place the scallions and grated ginger in small dishes on the table. Put a few tablespoons of tsuyu dipping sauce into a small bowl at each place setting. To eat, sprinkle the scallions and some grated ginger into the sauce, then dunk in the kakiage and noodles.

1 cup all-purpose flour

3 tablespoons cornstarch

1 teaspoon kosher salt

1¼ cups cold seltzer, plus more as needed

2 ice cubes

1 yellow onion, thinly sliced

1 ear corn, kernels cut off the cob

1 red bell pepper, sliced into thin strips

¼ cup green peas or shelled edamame (fresh or frozen)

Canola or vegetable oil, for frying

14 ounces dried soba noodles, or 16 ounces fresh

2 scallions, thinly sliced

Finely grated fresh ginger, about 1 teaspoon per serving

Tsuyu (Dashi-Soy Dipping Sauce, page 122)

Hotpot and Tabletop Cooking

鍋と卓上料理

Tabletop cooking is common in Japan and is a fun, interactive way to share a meal. For us, that means setting up a grill outside for yakiniku (Japanese barbecue) in warmer weather, or gathering around a hotpot during the cooler months. There's a dizzying array of ingredients waiting to get dunked, grilled, or simmered. When everyone is involved, there's a chaotic dance to it, with people reaching over one another, putting in morsels of food at different times, and fishing them out when they're done to their liking. We're all cooking together, but everyone gets to be their own chef.

How to Hotpot

Hotpot, also known as nabe, is less of a recipe and more of a philosophy. In Japan, hotpot is a winter family meal. You gather together around the steaming pot at the center of the table, taking time to enjoy the aromas and flavors of each ingredient as you cook it. The flavor of the broth also evolves as the meal progresses, making each hotpot experience unique.

The basic idea is this: You start with a simple pot of simmering broth and dip in an array of ingredients to cook them, hence the name hotpot. You can put almost anything in a hotpot, but the meal usually includes an assortment of meat, seafood, vegetables, and tofu, and ends with a starch, such as rice or noodles. The ingredients we've included in the following guide are our go-tos, but feel free to get creative and find the combinations that you like best.

We also include suggestions for the best way to cut ingredients, and which to leave whole. Hotpot is a great way to use up odds and ends, or an excuse to go out and get something special. Since it's tabletop cooking, most of the work is in preparing the ingredients, an important step that will allow everyone to enjoy the meal once it's started.

Our guidelines to making hotpot at home:

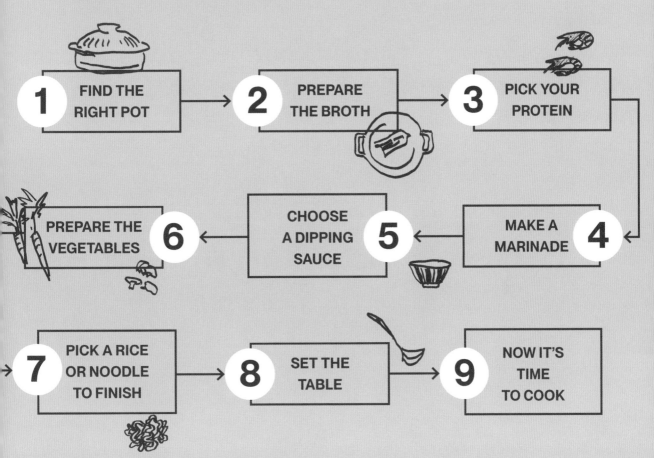

1 FIND THE RIGHT POT → 2 PREPARE THE BROTH → 3 PICK YOUR PROTEIN

6 PREPARE THE VEGETABLES ← 5 CHOOSE A DIPPING SAUCE ← 4 MAKE A MARINADE

7 PICK A RICE OR NOODLE TO FINISH → 8 SET THE TABLE → 9 NOW IT'S TIME TO COOK

1 → FIND THE RIGHT POT

You want a pot with a lid. We use a donabe pot, a Japanese earthenware pot with a heavy lid that is typically used for one-pot dishes and is safe to use on a stovetop (see Sources, page 252). If you don't have a pot like this, you can use an enameled cast-iron braiser or Dutch oven like Le Creuset or Staub, or even a regular pot. A 2-quart pot is a good size for a family of four.

2 → PREPARE THE BROTH

Fill the pot three-quarters full with either Dashi (page 33) or with water and a 4-inch square of kombu. Let the kombu soak while you prepare the other ingredients. As it sits, it adds more umami and body to the water.

3 → PICK YOUR PROTEIN

It's great to mix and match proteins in a hotpot: pork and clams, oysters and beef, shrimp and chicken, crab and fish, different kinds of tofu (silken, fried)—the possibilities are endless and no two hotpot experiences are the same (for some of our favorite combinations, see Sample Hotpots on page 149). Think about what you have in the fridge and the freezer, or make a trip to the store for something special. Generally, we prepare 4 to 6 ounces of protein per person. Prepare a large platter that can fit all of your proteins. These are the ones we use most.

BEEF

Rib eye or sirloin: No matter the type of beef you buy, you want the cut to be tender because you're cooking it quickly (this is a great preparation for wagyu beef, if you want to splurge). We like to buy the super-thin, quick-cooking, presliced meat from the Asian grocer, but also give instructions on how to slice it yourself (see Buying and Slicing Meat, page 148).

CHICKEN

We use both thigh and breast, with skin on or off, and we cut breasts into ½-inch slices and thighs into 1- or 2-inch chunks for ease of cooking. For even more flavor, try raw chicken meatballs (Tsukune, page 187), dropped by the spoonful directly into the pot.

PORK

Shoulder or belly: Any cut with good fat content, sliced very thin, adds a nice pork fat flavor to the broth. We like to use high-quality heritage pork, such as Kurobuta (Berkshire).

Sausage: Try kielbasa or bratwurst, cut into bite-size pieces, or fresh sausage squeezed out of the casing into little nuggets.

SEAFOOD

FISH

Sea bass, cod, snapper, salmon . . . just about any fish will work. Start with a fillet and cut into 2- to 3-inch pieces, slightly larger than bite-size since fish cooks quickly and flakes apart easily once cooked. Enjoy it plain or marinated.

SHELLFISH

Shrimp: Cook head-on for maximum flavor, shell-on for medium flavor, or peeled for convenience. Any size will work.

Clams (littleneck, top neck, Manila, or cockles): Soak in a bowl of salty water and refrigerate overnight to purge of sand. Drain before using. Add to the hotpot and cook until they open. A handful will add excellent flavor to the broth, and complement other proteins, like fish, sausage, or pork.

Oysters: Shuck and add to the hotpot with their liquor. We love to pair them with beef, but oysters alone can be the star.

4 ⟶ **MAKE A MARINADE**

These three simple marinades can be used interchangeably with chicken, pork, fish, and tofu. (We typically don't marinate beef.) Marinate for a minimum of 15 minutes or up to a day.

Sake Marinade: For each 1 pound of chicken, pork, fish, or tofu, marinate with ¼ cup sake, a few thin slices of ginger, 1 or 2 halved garlic cloves, and 2 scallions, cut into 2-inch pieces.

Shio Koji Marinade: For each 1 pound of chicken, pork, fish, or tofu, pour over 3 tablespoons shio koji and massage it in.

Miso Marinade: For each 1 pound of chicken, pork, fish, or tofu, marinate with 2 teaspoons sake, 2 teaspoons mirin, and 3 tablespoons miso. For a sweeter marinade use saikyo shiro (white) miso, and for a saltier version use a darker (aka or awase) miso.

5 ⟶ **CHOOSE A DIPPING SAUCE**

Dipping sauces complement the flavors of the ingredients in the hotpot, seasoning both them and the broth. The one we use the most is citrusy Ponzu (page 36). It goes perfectly with seafood and unctuous meats. We also enjoy sesame dipping sauce (recipe follows), though we use it more sparingly, often in conjunction with the ponzu. Since it's rich, it goes well with leaner ingredients like tofu and vegetables.

Sesame Dipping Sauce: In a small bowl, thoroughly combine ½ cup tahini, 3 tablespoons rice vinegar, ¼ cup soy sauce, 1 tablespoon sugar, and 3 tablespoons water. Refrigerate until ready to use. It can keep for months in the refrigerator. Makes 1 cup.

6 ⟶ **PREPARE THE VEGETABLES**

Regardless of the protein we're cooking, we always include the following vegetables in the hotpot. Feel free to mix and match, or choose the ones you like best. We serve about a generous salad's worth per person.

Napa cabbage: Take a few leaves (2 to 3 per person), layer them on top of each other, cut it in half lengthwise down the rib, and then slice on the diagonal into 1-inch pieces.

Mushrooms: For shiitake, discard the stems and score a plus sign into the mushroom cap, so the mushrooms absorb more of the broth and give off more flavor. For maitake, shimeji, or enoki mushrooms, tear them into bite-size clusters.

Tokyo negi or leeks: Cut into 2-inch lengths, using only the white parts.

Daikon radish and carrot: Cut the daikon into tanzaku (see page 31). Cut the carrot crosswise on the diagonal into ¼-inch slices.

Quick-cooking greens: Shungiku (chrysanthemum greens), mizuna, komatsuna (Japanese spinach), spinach, bok choy, or kale all work well. Wash thoroughly and leave whole or cut into bite-size pieces.

Tofu: We always include soft or silken tofu on our vegetable platter, cut into matchbox-size pieces.

Malony (aka glass noodles): These translucent dried noodles made of potato starch are popular in hotpot cooking. Precook for 2 minutes in boiling water, drain in a colander, run under cold water until cooled, shake off any excess water and chill until ready to use.

7 ⟶ PICK A RICE OR NOODLE TO FINISH

Shime and *shiage* both mean "finish" in Japanese. In the context of hotpot, these words refer to the starch course that ends the meal. We choose either udon noodles or rice to cook in the broth, which has been flavored by the proteins and vegetables that were cooked in it. A cup or two of cooked rice or one to two servings of noodles should be plenty to finish out a hotpot meal, unless you're a sumo wrestler or a growing teenager.

Udon: If beef, pork, or chicken is the star of the pot, we prefer finishing with udon. The noodles should be cooked ahead of time, according to the package directions (see How to Cook Japanese Noodles, page 124).

Rice: We choose rice for a hotpot with chicken, seafood, or pork. The rice should be cooked, but it can be day-old rice or thawed rice from the freezer. By adding rice to the broth, it becomes congee. We like to add a beaten egg right before serving.

8 ⟶ SET THE TABLE

What you want on the table for your hotpot meal:

Butane burner: This burner (see page 29) allows us to cook on the tabletop. A hot plate could also work. If you don't have a burner, cook on the stove and bring it to the table (see How to Cook on the Stovetop, below).

Ladles (see page 30)

Cooking chopsticks (see page 29)

A **bowl** and **chopsticks** at each place setting

Vegetable platter

Protein platter

Rice or noodles, plus one egg if using rice

Condiments:

- Dipping sauce(s)
- Thinly sliced scallions
- Julienned lemon or yuzu zest
- Grated daikon radish
- Yuzu kosho
- Salt
- Ground toasted sesame seeds

How to Cook on the Stovetop

Bring a pot three-quarters full of dashi or water and kombu to a boil over medium-high heat. Add as many vegetables as you can fit in the pot without overcrowding, return to a boil, then simmer for a few minutes. Add the protein(s), cook, and bring to the table to eat. Repeat as needed with the remaining ingredients. For the shime, bring the pot back to the stovetop and follow the directions in step 7, above.

9 → NOW IT'S TIME TO COOK

For some of our favorite combinations, see Sample Hotpots on page 149.

Make the broth: Bring the pot with dashi or water and kombu to a simmer over medium-high heat on the tabletop burner. You want to keep it at a nice gentle simmer, adjusting the heat accordingly to maintain it.

Prepare the condiments in your bowl: Pour in ponzu sauce, sprinkle on some scallions and citrus zest, and add ground sesame seeds. We prefer adding grated daikon only if we have a sweet daikon (some daikon can be too spicy). You can add yuzu kosho for heat. Replenish as you go. If using sesame sauce, pour in a bowl, and sprinkle on some scallions and citrus zest if you like.

First we eat the tofu: Drop the tofu into the hot water and let it warm up for a few minutes, then put it in your bowl with the condiments and eat it.

Next, add other ingredients to build the hotpot: Start with things that take the longest to cook, such as Tokyo negi or leek, daikon, carrot, mushrooms, and the thick part of the napa cabbage. Increase the heat to high, put the lid on and cook until you can hear that it's boiling, 4 or 5 minutes.

Remove the lid, reduce the heat and start adding the protein: If using thinly sliced beef or pork, lay a few pieces on top at a time and cook until the meat is done to your liking, about 30 seconds. If using seafood or poultry, cook for a little longer. Start eating as things are done cooking. Repeat as you wish. Add the malony whenever you want some noodles, and let cook for a few minutes before eating. You can also add some broth to your bowl as it starts to develop flavor. During the cooking process, if the liquid is looking too low, you can add more dashi or water.

There are no rules at this point—eat and cook as much as you would like! Sometimes, we push the cooked vegetables to one side of the hotpot and add the fresh vegetables to the other side, or we take everything out and start again. Over time, you'll develop your own hotpot style. Just leave a little room for your *shime*, or starch "finish."

For the shime: You want about half of the cooking liquid you started with. If using udon, which should already be cooked, add it to the pot and boil to heat through. Transfer it to your dish and season with salt, more ponzu, or whatever you have left in your bowl. When using cooked rice, mix it into the broth and let it simmer a bit to absorb the liquid. Beat an egg in a small bowl and pour it in a thin stream over the rice in a circular motion, swirling it in. If you have scallions left over, sprinkle them over the egg and close the lid for 1 minute. Turn the heat off. Open the lid, ladle the rice into your bowl, and season with salt or ponzu.

Buying and Slicing Meat

The Japanese grocery store usually sells thinly presliced beef or pork, cut about 1/16 to 1/8 inch thick, in the freezer or refrigerated section.

If you can't find presliced beef, buy a piece of meat, put it in the freezer until it is semifrozen, and slice against the grain as thin as you can get it, aiming for 1/16 to 1/8 inch. If slicing doesn't get you there, take a slice of meat, place it on a cutting board, put a piece of parchment over it and roll it out with a rolling pin, or gently pound it with a meat mallet, to the desired thickness. For hotpot, it's also okay to just cut the meat into bite-size pieces. It will take longer to cook, but it will still be delicious.

When shopping for Japanese beef, known as wagyu, generally you will find two kinds: beef from cattle raised in Japan (pictured below), and beef from cattle raised domestically. Both are delicious but have distinct characteristics.

Japanese wagyu is highly marbled and very expensive. The beef is named for where it's from. Kobe is the most famous variety in this country, but great beef is produced throughout Japan. Japan has a unique way of grading its beef. A5, the highest grade that refers to how much fat is marbled throughout the meat, is the most common kind of Japanese beef you will see imported here. It's melt-in-your mouth tender, and you don't need to eat a lot of it to feel satiated.

American Wagyu is an extremely flavorful hybrid of premium Japanese and American cattle. Though it's less marbled than Japanese beef, it's still incredibly high-quality, drawing off of the two best traits of American beef (meaty and flavorful) and Japanese beef (tender and beautifully marbled). It's still very expensive, but more affordable than Japanese wagyu. There is also a wider variety of cuts available.

Sample Hotpots

When we make hotpot, the type of broth and the assortment of vegetables and seasonings that we use generally don't change. But we like to mix up the proteins depending on the occasion. The more celebratory the meal, the more we're likely to spend. For a low-key weeknight hotpot, we might go with something like marinated chicken. For a special dinner, we'll buy pork belly and clams, or splurge on expensive Japanese beef and oysters. Whether we finish with noodles or rice depends mostly on our mood. Below are the ingredients you'll need to make some of our favorite hotpots, ranging from simple to luxurious. To cook them, follow the directions in Now It's Time to Cook (page 147). **Serves 4 to 6**

→ THE BROTH

4-inch square of kombu

Pot filled ¾ full with water

→ THE VEGETABLE PLATTER

12 napa cabbage leaves, halved lengthwise down the rib, and sliced on the diagonal into 1-inch pieces

8 shiitake mushrooms caps, with a plus sign scored into the top of each

1 small bunch maitake or shimeji mushrooms, torn into bite-size clusters

2 large Tokyo negi or leeks, white part only, cleaned and cut into 2-inch pieces

1 large carrot, peeled and cut on the diagonal into ¼-inch-thick slices

8 ounces daikon radish, peeled, cut into tanzaku (see page 31)

1 bunch shungiku (chrysanthemum greens), mizuna, komatsuna (Japanese spinach), spinach, bok choy, or kale, rinsed thoroughly

1 (14-ounce) package of silken or soft tofu, cut into matchbox-size pieces

8 ounces malony (glass noodles), parcooked for 2 minutes in boiling water and chilled until ready to use

→ PICK A PROTEIN *(choose one combination for your hotpot)*

SIMPLE MARINATED CHICKEN HOTPOT
1 to 1½ pounds boneless chicken, dark and/or white meat, preferably skin on, cut into bite-size pieces. Marinate in a Sake Marinade (page 145) for 15 minutes or up to overnight.

OR

SHIO KOJI SEA BASS HOTPOT
1 to 1½ pounds black sea bass fillet, skin on, pin bones removed. Cut the fillets into 3 or 4 pieces. Marinate in Shio Koji Marinade (page 145) for 15 minutes or up to overnight.

OR

PORK BELLY AND CLAM HOTPOT
1 to 1½ pounds thinly sliced pork belly or shoulder and 12 littleneck clams, soaked in salty water overnight in the refrigerator to purge of sand and scrubbed clean

OR

BEEF AND OYSTER HOTPOT
1 to 1½ pounds premium Japanese beef, thinly sliced (see Buying and Slicing Meat, opposite) and 12 oysters, shucked

→ THE SHIME (FINISH)

1 pound frozen or ½ pound dried udon noodles (such as Inaniwa, Sanuki, or Sanuki-style) or somen noodles, cooked according to package directions (see page 124)

OR 2 cups cooked Japanese White Rice (page 215)

→ SEASONING AND GARNISH

4 scallions, thinly sliced	Ponzu Sauce (page 36)	1 (2- to 3-ounce) jar yuzu kosho
Julienned lemon or yuzu zest	Ground, toasted sesame seeds	

Rib Eye Sukiyaki

すき焼き

Sukiyaki Sauce
¾ cup sake
¾ cup mirin
¼ cup sugar
¾ cup soy sauce

Sukiyaki
6-inch piece gobo
  (burdock root)
1 pound frozen or ½ pound
  dried udon noodles
4 ounces shirataki or
  konnyaku noodle
1 large leek, white part only,
  cleaned and cut into
  1½-inch pieces
4 shiitake caps, halved
1 fist-size cluster shimeji
  (beech) mushrooms, torn
  into 6 to 8 small clusters
1 carrot, peeled and cut into
  tanzaku (see page 31)
4 ounces daikon radish,
  peeled, cut into tanzaku
8 napa cabbage leaves,
  split down the middle
  and cut crosswise into
  2-inch strips
5 ounces soft tofu, cut into
  matchbox-size pieces
4 ounces shungiku
  (chrysanthemum greens),
  spinach, or Swiss chard
1 pound thinly sliced rib eye
  (see Buying and Slicing
  Meat, page 148)
4 eggs, preferably farm-fresh
1 2-inch cube of beef fat or
  2 tablespoons canola oil

When I was little, my mother served sukiyaki on special occasions. It's a hotpot meal cooked right at the table, a quick braise of thinly sliced beef, vegetables, and tofu flavored with sake, sugar, and soy sauce. We'd pluck hot pieces of meat straight from the pot while my mom would add more, dipping the beef into a sauce of raw egg, which cooled and coated each bite.

Eating sukiyaki is interactive and fun. The burner is at the center of the action, along with the sauce and platters with prepped ingredients. Once in the pot, they should be arranged in little groups, not mixed together like a stir-fry. This way of organizing helps keep track of how long they've been cooking, and it's prettier. As the ingredients cook down, keep the clusters together, pulling them out as they're ready to eat, and shuffling them aside to make room for more. At the end, finish with the noodles.

If you don't have a butane burner, you can cook sukiyaki on the stovetop and bring the pot to the table. After most of the items are eaten, return the pot to the stove to cook the udon, then bring it back to the table to feast. —**Sawa**

SERVES 4 · TOTAL TIME: 1½ HOURS

To make the sukiyaki sauce: In a small pot, bring the sake, mirin, sugar, and soy sauce to a boil over high heat. Stir a few times to dissolve the sugar, then boil until the alcohol is cooked off, about 2 minutes. Transfer to a heatproof container. The sauce can keep, covered, for up to 1 month in the refrigerator.

To prepare the sukiyaki: Fill a bowl halfway with cold water. Scrub off most of the brown outer layer of the gobo using a tawashi or a vegetable brush. Cut on the diagonal into ¼-inch-thick slices and drop in the water immediately to prevent oxidation. Set aside.

Bring a large pot of water to a boil for the noodles.

Drop the udon noodles into the boiling water and cook according to the package directions (see How to Cook Japanese Noodles, page 124). Drain in a colander and run under cold water until cooled. Place the colander over a bowl and set aside.

Bring a small pot of water to a boil for the shirataki. Add the shirataki and blanch for 3 minutes to remove any odor from the packaging. Drain and set aside.

Arrange the shirataki, leek, shiitake, shimeji mushrooms, carrot, daikon, napa cabbage, tofu, and shungiku in clusters on a platter and bring to the table. Place the beef and udon noodles on separate plates.

continued

Set up the butane burner in the center of the table following the manufacturer's instructions.

Set everyone up with a soup bowl (four total) and have each person crack an egg into their bowl, then lightly beat with chopsticks.

Set a large cast-iron skillet (or enameled cast-iron braiser such as Le Creuset) on the butane burner and heat the beef fat over medium-high heat, moving it around frequently. After a few minutes, the pan should look shiny, and there should be about a tablespoon of melted fat. Reduce the heat to medium and add the leeks, turning occasionally, until golden on all sides, 5 to 6 minutes.

Drain the gobo in a colander and shake to get the excess water off. Shuffle the leeks to one side of the pot and add the gobo to the center. Increase the heat to high and cook to get rid of the excess liquid, 2 to 3 minutes. When you hear the gobo start to sizzle, add about half of the sukiyaki sauce, then shuffle the gobo to the side of the pot next to the leeks. (During cooking, the ingredients should always be simmering in ¼ to ½ inch of liquid. If the liquid reduces too much and the pot starts to dry out, add more sauce or some water.)

Now add about half each of the shiitake and shimeji mushrooms, carrots, daikon, napa cabbage, tofu, and shirataki, each in its own cluster. The pot should look full. Turn the heat to medium-high, cover, and cook until the cabbage is soft, 4 to 6 minutes. Uncover, make a little more room on one side, add the shungiku, and cook until wilted, 1 to 2 minutes. Lay as many beef slices as you can fit in a single layer over the other ingredients and cook gently, spooning on some of the sauce until it starts to turn rosy pink, 1 to 2 minutes. Make room in the pan for the cooked beef and put it together in a cluster.

Eat the vegetables and beef straight out of the pot, dipping them into the raw egg sauce. Add more vegetables and beef to the pot as space opens up, pushing everything that is cooked to one side, and using the other side for cooking. Add more sauce for seasoning if needed, or a few tablespoons of water if the flavor is too concentrated. Once the pot is empty (or has enough room), add the udon noodles, the remaining sauce, and a tablespoon or two of water, about ¼ cup of liquid total. Cook over medium heat just to heat the noodles through, 3 to 4 minutes. The starch from the noodles will thicken the sauce and coat the noodles. Eat immediately, or take your time. The noodles will soften and absorb more flavor as they cook.

Oden is a hearty, satisfying hotpot meal that's easy to make, and perfumes your home with savory aromas of dashi and chicken stock. It's substantial without being heavy, perfect when nights get chilly. Chock-full of potatoes, daikon radish, carrots, chicken, eggs, and a variety of fish cakes (see page 155), it has something for everyone. Best of all, it lasts for days, nourishing us for many meals. If you don't have chicken stock, you can just use all dashi for the braising liquid and it will still be delicious. The braised daikon in this dish is particularly satisfying. Scoring a shallow X into the top helps the daikon absorb the broth and transform from crunchy and mildly spicy to silky and sweet. Like most stews, it's always better on the second day, and gets tastier each time we reheat it. —Aaron

SERVES 4 TO 6 • ACTIVE TIME: 30 MINUTES • TOTAL TIME: 1 HOUR 45 MINUTES

In a large pot (at least 8-quart) or a braiser with a lid, heat the oil over medium heat for 2 minutes. Season the chicken thighs with 1 teaspoon of the salt, place skin-side down in the pot, and cook until the fat melts out and the skin becomes golden and crispy, 5 to 7 minutes. Flip over and pour in the mirin and sake. Increase the heat to high, bring to a boil, and cook until the liquid is reduced by half, about 3 minutes. Add the chicken stock, dashi, the remaining 1 tablespoon salt, the soy sauce, ginger, shiitake, carrot, potatoes, and daikon and bring to a boil. Skim off any foam that comes to the surface to help keep the broth clear. Reduce the heat to low, cover, and gently simmer for 20 minutes.

Meanwhile, bring a small pot of water to a boil over high heat. Drop in the konnyaku, return to a boil, and cook for 3 minutes. Drain and add to the pot.

Put the eggs in a small pot. Cover with water and bring to a boil over high heat. Adjust the heat to a low simmer and cook for 8 minutes. Drain, transfer to a small bowl, and run under cold water. Once they're cool enough to handle, peel and add to the stew pot.

When the stew has simmered for the 20 minutes, add the fish cakes (unless you are using hanpen, which should be added during the last few minutes of cooking) and mochi kinchaku (if using). Continue to simmer until the carrots, potatoes, and daikon are cooked and a cake tester or tip of a knife goes in with no resistance, about 25 minutes. If cooking hanpen, add at this stage and simmer until soft and spongy, 2 to 3 minutes.

continued

Oden

おでん

1 tablespoon canola oil or other neutral oil

4 bone-in, skin-on chicken thighs (small or medium)

1 tablespoon plus 1 teaspoon kosher salt

½ cup mirin

½ cup sake

4 cups chicken stock

4 cups Dashi (page 33) or 4 teaspoons dashi powder mixed into 4 cups water

1 tablespoon soy sauce

1-inch piece of fresh ginger, halved

4 large shiitake mushroom caps, halved

1 large carrot, peeled and cut into 2-inch lengths

½ pound Yukon Gold potatoes (about 2 potatoes), scrubbed clean and quartered

12 ounces daikon radish, peeled, cut into 2-inch chunks, and scored on one side with an "X" ¼ inch deep

1 (8-ounce) brick konnyaku, cut into ½-inch-thick slices

4 eggs

16 fish cakes, such as a mix of chikuwa, gobo-maki, satsuma-age, or hanpen (see Fish Cakes, page 155)

4 pieces mochi kinchaku (optional; see Note)

Karashi (Japanese mustard) or Dijon mustard, for serving

Set the table with the butane burner in the center. Put the pot on the burner and turn it on to the lowest setting to keep it warm, or just bring the pot to the table and set it in the center. Each person should ladle some broth into their bowl. Add the items from the pot that you want to eat. Swirl some mustard into the broth, or smear a bit onto the individual ingredients. If you find a piece of ginger, discard it. Oden will keep for up to 1 week in the refrigerator.

Note We like to put mochi kinchaku in our oden, which is aburaage (fried tofu skin) stuffed with mochi, a glutinous rice cake. You can purchase mochi kinchaku premade or assemble it yourself by cutting a rectangular piece of aburaage into 2 equal squares, stuffing each with a piece of mochi, and threading the ends with a toothpick to close.

FISH CAKES

The real star of oden are the fish cakes: seafood that's ground or pounded into a paste, bound with starch, and broiled, fried, or steamed. It's possible to make your own, but there are so many terrific ready-made versions at Japanese and Asian supermarkets (we like Kibun and Shirakiku brands, which are made in Japan). **Chikuwa** ❶ is a broiled fish cake in an easy-to-recognize tube-like shape. Fried fish cakes include **gobo-maki** ❷, a cylinder stuffed with a piece of burdock, and **satsuma-age** ❸, a disk or ball with vegetables, such as grated carrots or peas. If octopus is added, it's called **tako bolu** ❹ (octopus ball). Some fish cakes are boiled, like **yasai tsumire** ❺, a free-form fish cake with assorted vegetables, and **hanpen** ❻, a rectangular cake cut in half to make triangles that's light and fluffy from the grated nagaimo mixed in.

Yakiniku

Japanese Barbecue

焼き肉

Yakiniku Sauce

6 tablespoons soy sauce

2 tablespoons sake

¼ cup apple cider or juice

3 tablespoons sugar

1 tablespoon kimchi brine, or something else spicy and acidic, like hot sauce

2 tablespoons toasted sesame oil

1 tablespoon ground toasted sesame seeds

2-inch piece of fresh ginger, peeled and finely grated

2 garlic cloves, finely grated

¼ cup minced onion

Barbecue

1 pound short ribs, sliced ¼ inch thick (bone-in or boneless)

1 zucchini, cut into slices ½ inch thick

1 Japanese eggplant, cut into slices ½ inch thick

1 bunch scallions

12 shiitake mushroom caps

1 small onion, cut into 8 wedges

½ pound shishito peppers

1 head of green leaf lettuce, leaves separated

12 shiso leaves

Canola or other neutral oil in a squeeze bottle (or in bowl with a brush), for grilling

Cooked Japanese White Rice (page 215), for serving

No trip to Japan is complete without a night out at a yakiniku restaurant with old friends, cold beer, and some good laughs. It involves grilling platters of meat at the table, and some vegetables, too. In a large group it can be chaotic, raucous, smoky, and loads of fun.

Yakiniku often features all parts of the animal. When it comes to beef, you'll see prime cuts, as well as offal and tougher cuts that benefit from marinades, thin slicing, and quick cooking. An Asian grocer will often have meat already sliced for yakiniku or Korean barbecue. We use short rib in this recipe because we like how marbled and delicious it is, and you can buy it boneless and slice it yourself. But feel free to experiment with other cuts and meats. Skirt steak, hanger steak, sirloin, and rib eye are all good choices. Pork is also a great option, especially pork belly. If you see beef tongue, try it—it's one of our favorites. We don't recommend marinating it; just grill it with salt and squeeze on some lemon, like they do in Japan.

Because of the copious amount of smoke generated when grilling, yakiniku should not be done inside the home. We do our own version on our balcony. We set up a butane burner and a little grill pan and have fun cooking together, just like we do in Japan, but you can also do it on a conventional outdoor grill and just bring the food to the table.

SERVES 4 • ACTIVE TIME: 1 HOUR • TOTAL TIME: 1½ HOURS

To make the yakiniku sauce: In a 2-cup screw-top glass jar, combine the soy sauce, sake, apple cider, sugar, kimchi brine, sesame oil, ground sesame seeds, ginger, garlic, and onion. Screw on the lid and shake to mix. Refrigerate for up to 1 month.

Prepare the barbecue: Put the short ribs on a plate. Shake the yakiniku sauce well, then measure ¼ cup and pour over the short ribs, coating thoroughly. Marinate the ribs in the refrigerator for at least 30 minutes and up to 24 hours before grilling.

Arrange the zucchini, eggplant, scallions, mushrooms, onion, and shishito peppers on a large platter. Put the lettuce and shiso leaves on another.

Set the butane burner and grill pan outdoors in the center of a table. Place the marinated meat, platter of vegetables, plate of lettuce and shiso, and the remaining yakiniku sauce with a small spoon on the table. Prepare an empty plate on which to place the items as they come off the grill.

continued

Heat the grill pan on the burner over high heat (see Note). Squeeze about 2 teaspoons of oil onto the pan and carefully rub with a folded paper towel to lightly grease the surface. Grill the short ribs, zucchini, eggplant, scallions, mushrooms, onion, and shishito peppers, taking care to not overcrowd. Each ingredient takes a different amount of time to cook, but a good rule of thumb is to flip each item over once it has taken on some char or grill marks, 1 to 2 minutes, then grill the other side. Put the cooked items onto the prepared plate to be eaten as they come off the grill. Add more oil to the grill as necessary. Spoon yakiniku sauce over the meat and vegetables before eating, and wrap in lettuce leaves and shiso. Serve with white rice.

Note When using a butane burner with a grill pan, make sure the grill pan is the same size as the burner and does not hang over where the fuel canister is located. It can get hot, which is a safety hazard.

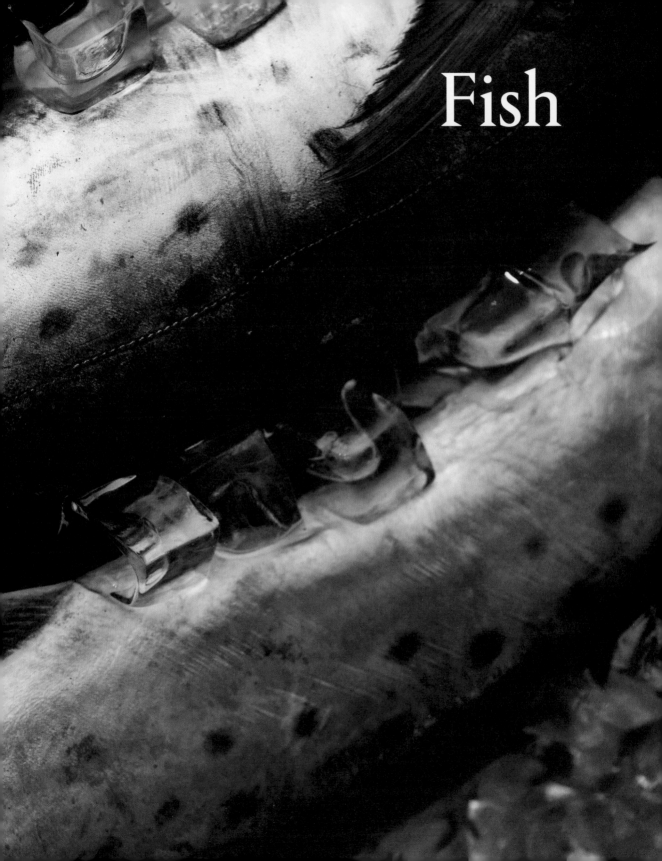

Fish

魚

Japan has a long tradition of eating fish; it's part of the culture. There are different seasons for different fish. Some are only available when they're at their peak flavor, or when they are passing through the local waters. Raw preparations like sushi are reserved for when the fish is the freshest, but fish is also enjoyed cured, pickled like escabeche, or broiled until the skin is bubbling and crackling. In Brooklyn, we go to the farmers' market to buy locally caught fish. We'll eat the best of what we find raw that day, buy some to cook the next day, and maybe cure or pickle the rest for later in the week.

Lox is a quintessential Jewish delicacy, but I learned from Sawa years ago that there's a long tradition of curing and smoking all kinds of fish in Japan. Though this recipe is technically for gravlax, an unsmoked style of cured salmon, we achieve the signature "lox" flavor by curing it with bonito flakes (shavings of dried smoked bonito), an effective way to infuse the fish with smoky flavor without having to cold smoke it.

Making your own lox is easy, rewarding, and much cheaper than buying it. When we shop for salmon, we look for organic or sustainably farmed fish. As much as we enjoy wild-caught salmon, farmed varieties have a higher fat content, which produces luscious, silkier lox. We find that king salmon or steelhead, which is technically a type of trout, produce the best results.

Bonito-cured lox takes 3 days to make, so if you want it for brunch on Saturday, be sure to get it going by Wednesday. Lox end pieces are great broiled and eaten for breakfast as Shiozake (page 54). We recommend soaking them in water for about 1 hour to pull out some of the salt; just pat it dry before broiling. **—Aaron**

SERVES 8 TO 10 • ACTIVE TIME: 30 MINUTES • TOTAL TIME: 3 DAYS, INCLUDING CURING TIME

To make the curing salt, in a bowl, mix together the salt, sugar, coriander, black pepper, and garlic, rubbing the garlic in with your fingertips until well incorporated.

Place the salmon skin-side down in a large container with a tight-fitting lid, or on baking sheet lined with parchment paper. Rub a little more than half of the curing salt evenly onto the flesh side of the salmon. Place the dill, parsley, and bonito flakes on top. Carefully flip the salmon over. Rub the remaining curing salt evenly over the other side. Cover with the lid or wrap the baking sheet in plastic wrap and refrigerate for 2 days to cure.

Rinse the salt, herbs, and bonito flakes off the salmon. Thoroughly pat dry using paper towels. Wrap in parchment paper, then in plastic wrap, and refrigerate overnight before cutting. This helps the salt distribute evenly throughout the fillet.

Line a small baking sheet with a piece of parchment paper and set aside.

To cut the lox, use a long, sharp slicing knife. Start cutting at the head side, which is the thicker end of the fillet. Hold the knife at a 45-degree angle to the cutting board and slice away from your body using a gentle back-and-

continued

Bonito-Cured Lox

サーモンのかつお節〆

6 tablespoons kosher salt
2 tablespoons plus
    1½ teaspoons sugar
2 teaspoons coriander seeds,
    toasted and coarsely
    ground
½ teaspoon black
    peppercorns, toasted
    and coarsely ground
1 small garlic clove, finely
    grated
1½- to 2-pound skin-on
    salmon fillet, preferably
    king salmon or steelhead,
    pin bones removed
½ small bunch dill, rinsed
    and dried
½ small bunch curly parsley,
    rinsed and dried
1 cup bonito flakes

forth sawing motion. Make sure to follow all the way through until the slice is completed. Try and make the slices as thin as you possibly can while maintaining your angle—ideally, you want to see the blade through the slice while you're cutting. You'll need to make a few cuts before you're able to establish the angle and get slices that are consistent.

Transfer the slices to the lined baking sheet, placing them so they overlap slightly. When you've covered the whole piece of parchment with lox, place another sheet on top. Continue slicing until you have cut the entire fillet, or leave some unsliced and use it for Shiozake (page 54). Cover with a piece of parchment paper and wrap tightly in plastic. The lox will keep for up to 4 days in the refrigerator, or up to 1 month in the freezer.

CHOOSING SUSHI-QUALITY FISH

When it comes to selecting fish to eat raw, there are a few basic rules. First, look for what's freshest. A whole fish should look glossy, the eyes clear, and the gills bright red. If cut, the flesh should be vibrant, a little shiny, and slightly translucent. If there is a blood line (the part that is red on sea bass or yellowtail) it should be bright red, not dull or oxidized. If you can, pick up the fish. It should feel firm. The final test is smell. It should smell like the ocean, no fishy aromas.

A fish market you trust should be able to tell you what is safe to eat raw. Usually, local fish travels the shortest distance, and is therefore freshest and most suitable for sashimi. Japanese grocers that sell fish for sashimi will probably have a selection of fresh local fish, as well as fish that has been imported from Japan.

A few of our favorites are tuna (maguro), sea bass (suzuki), red snapper (tai), salmon (sake), fluke (hirame), and sea scallops (hotate). There are a few species to avoid no matter the quality: swordfish, monkfish, and cod can contain parasites, which aren't harmful when cooked, but are not okay eaten raw.

After you purchase the fish, keep it on ice for the journey home. Always purchase fish that you are going to eat raw on the day you plan to consume it. Last, if you don't see anything that looks good, then don't buy it! Go with something cooked; shrimp and crab are both great alternatives when making hand roll sushi (page 168).

The lox bowl was one of the first dishes we made in our journey toward creating a cuisine together. For a Jewish New Yorker, lox is something you put on a bagel, but for a Japanese person, cured fish and sushi rice make perfect sense. This recipe is a marriage of our sensibilities, a sort of free-form sushi with Ashkenazi flare. The components of the lox bowl are simple to make, and a few—the salmon, the chile mayo, and sweet kombu—can be prepared in advance. Though the dish requires some planning, it's well worth it. Once you have the ingredients ready to go, it comes together quickly.

SERVES 4 • TOTAL TIME: 1 HOUR 15 MINUTES

Distribute the rice equally among four shallow bowls. Cover in an even layer of lox, dividing the slices equally among them. Using a squeeze bottle or a spoon, drizzle the chile mayo over the lox.

Divide the avocado slices, sweet kombu, cucumber, pickles, capers, cilantro, scallions, ikura, and shredded nori equally among the bowls. You can arrange them whichever way you like, but we usually place them in clusters going clockwise: First the avocado, then the sweet kombu, followed by the cucumber and pickles. Sprinkle the capers and cilantro around the rim, and place the scallions and ikura in two mounds in the center. Crown them with the shredded nori and serve.

Lox Bowl

サーモンちらし

6 cups Sumeshi (Sushi Rice, page 217), freshly made

¾ to 1 pound store-bought lox or Bonito-Cured Lox (page 163), thinly sliced (about 16 slices)

2 to 4 tablespoons Chile Mayo (page 34), to taste

1 avocado, thinly sliced

Sweet Kombu (page 35)

1 small cucumber, preferably Japanese, cut into slices ⅛ inch thick

¼ cup assorted Japanese pickles, such takuan (yellow daikon) or kyurizuke (cucumber)

1 tablespoon capers, drained

½ bunch cilantro leaves, including some of the tender stems

2 scallions, thinly sliced

¼ cup ikura (salmon roe), or more to taste

¼ cup shredded nori, or a sheet of sushi nori cut into very thin strips using kitchen shears

Temaki Zushi

Hand Roll Sushi

手巻き寿司

Fillings

1 pound sushi-grade tuna,
  or a mix of high-quality
  sashimi fish (see Choosing
  Sushi-Quality Fish,
  page 165)
1 Tamagoyaki (page 42),
  cut in half, each half cut
  lengthwise into ½-inch-
  wide strips
1 cucumber, julienned
  (about 4 inches long)
1 avocado, sliced
8 to 12 shiso leaves,
  stems removed

For Serving

6 cups Sumeshi (Sushi Rice,
  page 217), freshly made
10 (7 × 8-inch) nori sheets,
  cut in half to make
  20 (7 × 4-inch) pieces
2 scallions, thinly sliced
Toasted sesame seeds
Gari (pickled ginger)
Wasabi paste
Chile Mayo (page 34)
Soy sauce

Temaki, or hand rolls, are a fun, casual way to make sushi at home. You just set out sushi rice, a platter of fillings, dishes of condiments, and sheets of nori, and everyone can roll their own.

We get our fish from a Japanese grocery store or a local fishmonger (see Choosing Sushi-Quality Fish, page 165). If you want to use cured fish, our Bonito-Cured Lox (page 163) works great. You can expand the variety of fillings beyond what we suggest in the recipe: Uni (sea urchin), ikura (salmon roe), or sweet shrimp are all nice additions. Vegetarians can use cooked mushrooms, asparagus, or blanched carrot strips.

We start by making sushi rice. While it's cooking, we prepare the fillings for the temaki. We start rolling as soon as the rice is ready, when it's still a little warm, and we never refrigerate it before using. If you don't use the rice immediately, you can leave it on the counter for a couple of hours covered with a damp towel to prevent it from drying out. **—Sawa**

MAKES ABOUT 20 TEMAKI (SERVES 4 TO 6) • TOTAL TIME: 1 HOUR

Prepare the fillings: Using a very sharp knife with a long blade, slice the fish into 2- to 3-inch pieces about ⅓ inch thick, or cut into 4-inch-long strips, about the same thickness.

Arrange the sliced fish, tamagoyaki, cucumber, avocado, and shiso leaves on a large platter. Cover with plastic wrap and refrigerate until you are ready to make the temaki, up to 4 hours ahead.

When ready to serve: Have the sushi rice ready at room temperature.

To set the table for the temaki, put a plate with the nori sheets, small dishes of scallions, toasted sesame seeds, gari, wasabi, and chile mayo, and a bottle of soy sauce on the table. Set each person up with a small plate for temaki and a smaller dish for soy sauce. Place the sushi rice on the table in a bowl. Prepare a rice paddle (or two) or a small wooden spoon in a container filled with water, which keeps the rice from sticking to the utensil.

To make temaki, put the piece of nori, smooth-side down, along the length of your hand, or widthwise on a plate. Dip the rice paddle in water, scoop about ⅓ cup of sushi rice and spread in a thin, even layer over the left half of the nori. Put a grain or two of rice on the bottom right corner of the nori ❶, which will help the nori stick to itself when you make the cone. Place the fillings on a diagonal over the rice, pointing toward the top left corner. Fold the bottom left corner over the rice toward the center of the sheet (❷ and ❸), and wrap into a cone shape ❹. Dip in soy sauce and enjoy.

In Japan, this is a simple, satisfying meal that one would eat for breakfast, lunch, or dinner. When I was a child, my mom would buy a whole mackerel with the head on, salt it, and put it under the broiler. The skin would turn brown and crispy, and you'd smell the fresh, juicy flesh cooking. Fat would drip and burn—the aroma was irresistible. Everyone would get a piece of fish with bones, and my mom would help me carefully pick them out with my chopsticks. It was difficult to do, but when I got a really good bite of fish and dipped it in the sharp daikon and tart ponzu sauce, it was like a reward.

When I can get my hands on fresh mackerel, this is my preferred way to cook it. For convenience, I usually cook fillets at home and season it, like my mom does, with good sea salt, then cook it under the broiler. Look for plump, firm mackerel that is glistening and slightly translucent. You don't want anything that looks floppy or dull. If mackerel isn't available, other oily fish such as porgy (also known as sea bream) and bluefish are good alternatives, as are black sea bass and striped bass. Cooking the fish with the skin on is key for this recipe. It gets great flavor in the broiler and acts as a barrier, insulating the moisture. Serve it with rice and you have a complete meal.

When you grate the daikon, you want to use the top part, toward the leaf, because it's sweeter. The tip tends to be spicier. **—Sawa**

SERVES 4 • TOTAL TIME: 10 MINUTES

Broiled Mackerel
with Grated Daikon and Ponzu

焼鯖とおろしぽん酢

2 skin-on Spanish mackerel
    fillets (8 to 12 ounces
    each), pin bones removed
2 teaspoons sea salt
1 cup grated daikon radish,
    on the medium-coarse
    holes of a box grater
Ponzu (page 36) or soy
    sauce and lemon juice,
    for serving
Cooked Japanese White Rice
    (page 215), for serving

Position an oven rack about 6 inches from the broiler element and preheat the broiler to high. Line a baking sheet with foil and lay the mackerel fillets side by side, skin-side down. Season with 1 teaspoon of the sea salt, flip over so the skin side is up, and season with the remaining 1 teaspoon salt.

Broil until the skin is bubbling and starts to char a bit, 4 to 6 minutes. Remove from the oven to check for doneness. If a fillet feels just delicate enough that it will fall apart with a gentle touch of your finger, then it is done. If it gives resistance, put the fish back under the broiler and cook for another minute. Remove the mackerel from the oven once it is cooked and immediately transfer to a serving platter.

To serve, divide the grated daikon among four small dishes, pour some ponzu on top (or drizzle with soy and add a squeeze of lemon), and eat each bite of mackerel with the ponzu-soaked daikon. Serve with rice.

Braised Black Sea Bass
with Ginger and Scallions

スズキの生姜煮

4 skin-on black sea bass
  fillets (6 ounces each),
  pin bones removed
1 teaspoon kosher salt
¼ cup sake
2 tablespoons soy sauce
1 tablespoon mirin
2 teaspoons sugar
½ cup water
1 tablespoon finely grated
  fresh ginger
4 scallions, thinly sliced
4 sprigs of cilantro, roughly
  chopped
Cooked Japanese White Rice
  (page 215), for serving

This is one of those dishes we make when we don't have much time on our hands but want something quick, healthy, and deeply satisfying. The soy-mirin braising liquid is a great sauce spooned over some rice, and the freshly grated ginger complements the dish's savory and sweet flavors. We like to use black sea bass for this, which has a beautiful, delicate texture and mild flavor, but you can do this preparation with just about any fish fillet, including red snapper, branzino, porgy, and sole. If you get a fillet that's thicker than ½ inch, increase the cooking time by 1 minute per ¼ inch of thickness. Scoring the fish skin with a sharp knife helps it cook faster and makes a beautiful presentation.

SERVES 4 • TOTAL TIME: 30 MINUTES

To score the skin of the fillets, make a diagonal slit about 2 inches long and ¼ inch deep every few inches, so you have 3 to 4 slits per fillet. Season with the salt and let sit for at least 15 minutes, up to overnight (cover and refrigerate if letting sit for more than 15 minutes). This step will season the fish and make it more flavorful.

In a 14-inch pan with a lid or a similar-size shallow enameled cast-iron braiser such as Staub or Le Creuset, combine the sake, soy sauce, mirin, sugar, and the ½ cup water and bring to a boil over high heat, stirring a few times to dissolve the sugar. Reduce the heat to medium and cook for 2 minutes to burn off the alcohol.

Divide the grated ginger equally among the fish fillets and spread evenly over the skin side. Place the fillets skin-side up in the pan and sprinkle with the scallions. Cover and cook for 3 minutes. Do not open the lid. Remove from the heat and let sit for another 3 minutes to allow the fish to continue to steam gently. Remove the lid; the fish should be opaque, and if you press it gently with your finger it should feel like it is going to flake apart. If it doesn't, cover for another 2 minutes. Sprinkle with the cilantro and serve immediately with cooked white rice.

There's something so satisfying about tearing open a crinkly parchment pouch at the table to reveal a beautiful meal inside. In this case, it's gently cooked flounder with tender mushrooms in a citrusy sauce of butter, sake, and umami-rich shio koji. Aside from the big reveal, cooking dinner in a pouch is a double win. It's a great way to prepare a meal ahead of time: When you're ready to eat, just pop the preassembled pouches in the oven, and by the time you set the table, dinner will be served. It's also an excellent technique for cooking fish, particularly lean varieties like flounder, fluke, or sole. The pouch seals in the moisture, with the added bonus of producing its own sauce, which is spectacular spooned over rice. If you can't find flounder, sea bass, snapper, and salmon are all good substitutes.

SERVES 4 • TOTAL TIME: 30 MINUTES

Preheat the oven to 350°F.

Cut out four 12 × 16-inch pieces of parchment paper or foil. Fold the pieces in half so the seam runs down the middle and each half measures 12 × 8 inches.

Place a flounder fillet on one side of each sheet. Dividing evenly, top each fillet with the mushrooms, scallions, butter, shio koji, sake, and yuzu zest. Fold the other half of the parchment over the fillets and crimp the edges to seal the pouch tightly so no steam can escape. It should look like an empanada when you're done. (This can be done anytime on the day you plan to cook them. Just store in the refrigerator until ready to use.)

Place the pouches on a baking sheet and cook for 10 minutes. Remove from the oven and let rest for 5 minutes to ensure that the steam has done its job and the fish is cooked. Transfer the packets to four plates and serve with bowls of rice. Carefully cut open and enjoy.

Flounder in a Pouch
with Mushrooms and Koji Butter Sauce

カレイの麹バター包み焼き

4 flounder fillets
    (6 ounces each)
2 cups sliced shiitake
    mushroom caps, or
    cremini mushrooms,
    or maitake or shimeji
    mushrooms pulled apart
    into small clusters
½ cup sliced scallions, green
    parts only, cut crosswise
    on the diagonal
3 tablespoons unsalted
    butter, cubed
4 tablespoons shio koji
4 teaspoons sake
Finely grated zest of 1 yuzu
    or lemon
Cooked Japanese White Rice
    (page 215), for serving

Nanban-zuke

Japanese Escabeche

南蛮漬け

4 teaspoons sugar

4 teaspoons mirin

2 tablespoons plus
   2 teaspoons soy sauce

¼ cup rice vinegar

½ cup Dashi (page 33) or
   ½ teaspoon dashi powder
   mixed into ½ cup water

½ yellow onion,
   very thinly sliced

½ carrot, finely julienned

1½ pounds sea bass, salmon,
   hake, perch, or red
   snapper fillets, cut into
   8 pieces all roughly the
   same size (skin on or
   off is okay)

2 teaspoons kosher salt

Cornstarch, for dusting

Canola oil or other neutral
   oil, for shallow-frying

Cooked Japanese White Rice
   (page 215), for serving
   (optional)

Nanban-zuke was first brought to Japan by the Portuguese in the seventeenth century. Its roots are in escabeche, the classic Portuguese dish of fried and marinated seafood or meat. Nanban-zuke is an early example of yoshoku, or dishes originating from outside Japan that have been adapted to Japanese cuisine. Today, this dish is a standard for Japanese cooks. This technique is a tried-and-true way to preserve the freshness of fish, and is a great meal to prepare a day ahead. You'll get the best results if the fish sits in the sweet-and-sour marinade overnight to let the flavors seep in, but a few hours will do.

SERVES 4 • ACTIVE TIME: 30 MINUTES • TOTAL TIME: 3 HOURS TO OVERNIGHT

In a pot, combine the sugar, mirin, soy sauce, rice vinegar, and dashi and bring to a boil over medium heat. Add the onion and carrot, stir once or twice, and bring back to a boil. Remove from the heat and set the marinade aside to cool.

Season both sides of the fish with the salt and place on a large plate. Put cornstarch in a small fine-mesh sieve and, gently tapping the sides, lightly dust one side of the fish. Flip over and lightly dust the other side. Take care to dust evenly and coat thoroughly.

Line a large plate with paper towels. Pour about ¼ inch canola oil into a deep medium skillet or sauté pan and warm over medium heat. Test the temperature by dropping a pinch of cornstarch into it. If it starts to sizzle immediately, the oil is hot enough for frying.

Add 4 of the fish fillets (skin-side down if skin-on) without crowding and press down gently using a fish spatula so they don't curl. Fry until the edges start to turn golden brown, 4 to 5 minutes. Flip and cook until the flesh has just turned opaque and the fish is just cooked through, about 30 seconds longer. Transfer from the pan to the paper towel–lined plate. Repeat with the remaining fillets.

Put the cooked fish in a large casserole or baking dish in an even layer, so it fits snugly but doesn't overlap. Pour the marinade on top and refrigerate, covered, for at least 3 hours or up to overnight before serving. Serve cold or at room temperature. Plate individually or on a platter, with the marinade and vegetables spooned over the fillets, and serve with white rice. It will keep, covered in the refrigerator, for up to 4 days.

Tataki is a method of flash-cooking meat or fish on high heat, leaving the inside raw. This type of preparation is reserved for the most prime cuts, which are free of sinew and incredibly tender. For this recipe, we use the highest-quality tuna we can find. Look for tuna steaks with flesh that is slightly translucent and a little shimmering. Anything dull, grayish, or oxidized is not good. Yellowfin and bigeye tuna should be a deep red color, while albacore will have a pinkish hue.

In Japan, sesame and tuna is a classic combination, and for this dish, we mix kuro neri goma (black sesame paste), soy sauce, and honey in a sauce that's savory, salty, slightly sweet, and as easy as can be. Lemon adds that crucial bit of acid to balance the dish. If you can't find kuro neri goma, you can use tahini, though the jet-black color does look striking on the plate. This sauce is versatile and pairs beautifully with other proteins, such as chicken, as well as roasted vegetables.

SERVES 4 • TOTAL TIME: 20 MINUTES

Tuna Tataki
with Sesame Sauce

マグロのたたき黒胡麻ソース

2 tablespoons plus 2 teaspoons
    kuro neri goma (black
    sesame paste) or tahini
2 tablespoons honey
2 tablespoons soy sauce
1½ pounds sushi-grade tuna
    steak, 1½ inches thick
1 tablespoon olive oil
Salt and freshly ground
    black pepper
1 lemon, quartered

In a small bowl, mix together the kuro neri goma and honey. Slowly drizzle in the soy sauce, whisking until it's well combined. The sauce will look thin but will thicken as it sits. You can make this ahead of time—it keeps covered in the refrigerator for weeks. If making ahead, stir before using.

Heat a 10-inch cast-iron grill pan or cast-iron skillet over high heat until it's very hot. To test, a drop of water sprinkled in the pan should sizzle and evaporate immediately.

If using a grill pan: Brush the tuna lightly with the olive oil on both sides and season with salt and pepper. Place the tuna in the pan, cook for 30 seconds, then rotate 90 degrees and cook for 15 seconds to create crosshatch marks. Flip and repeat on the other side. You are looking to sear the tuna and get grill marks on the outside, while keeping the center rare. (Alternatively, cook the tuna on an outdoor grill over high heat using the same method.) Remove the tuna and let it rest for 2 minutes.

If using a skillet: Season the tuna on both sides with salt and pepper. Add the olive oil to the skillet and cook the first side until lightly browned, about 1 minute. Repeat on the second side. Both sides should be lightly browned and the center rare. Remove the tuna from the pan and let it rest for 2 minutes.

To serve, pour the sauce on a serving platter. Using the back of a spoon, start at the center and push outward to form a large circle. Cut the tuna into ¼-inch-thick slices and arrange on the sesame sauce. Garnish with the lemon and serve.

FISH ON A FISH PLATE

Every time we go to Japan, I seek out pottery. Sawa has to rein me in, reminding me that it's delicate, heavy, and we don't have enough room in our luggage or our apartment back home. Nevertheless, after each trip we come back with pieces that are special to us. I always find myself wandering into a shop with lovely handcrafted plates, bowls, or cups from some local artisan. Unique plateware has become part of how we serve our food at home.

The first time I was in Kyoto, Sawa and I met up with her old friend Azusa at the Nishiki Market, a place where you can find everything food-related: knives, tableware, locally produced pickles, amazing vegetables, and stalls with the most incredible fish. Azusa took us to a small restaurant in the back of one of those fish stalls, a tiny, bustling izakaya with impeccable sashimi, served on a beautiful handcrafted ceramic platter in the shape of a fish. I'm not sure why, but it struck me: fish on a fish plate. It made such perfect sense, and in addition to making me chuckle, reminded me of the joy of not just what you are eating, but what you are serving it on.

The experience sparked my interest in Japanese ceramics, a natural progression given my background studying and making art, including pottery (not to mention my love of Japanese food). Future trips included an excursion to Tobe on Shikoku Island, near where Sawa's grandmother was from. That's where they make tobeyaki, a sturdy porcelain distinguished with striking hand-painted cobalt blue patterns and designs. It's what Sawa's mom likes to use for everyday eating at home. Other trips have taken us to Bizen, located in Okayama prefecture, not far from Hiroshima, where Sawa is from. Bizen is known for bizenyaki, a very old unglazed style of ceramics.

It turns out, though, that handcrafted ceramic fish plates are harder to find in Japan than you might think. So, with Sawa's encouragement, and some inspiration from Japan, I reignited my love of working with clay. She signed me up for time at a ceramic studio in our neighborhood. I bought fifty pounds of clay and started hand-building after the kids would go to sleep. Since then, I've made dozens of pieces: platters, sake cups, and, of course, fish plates. —Aaron

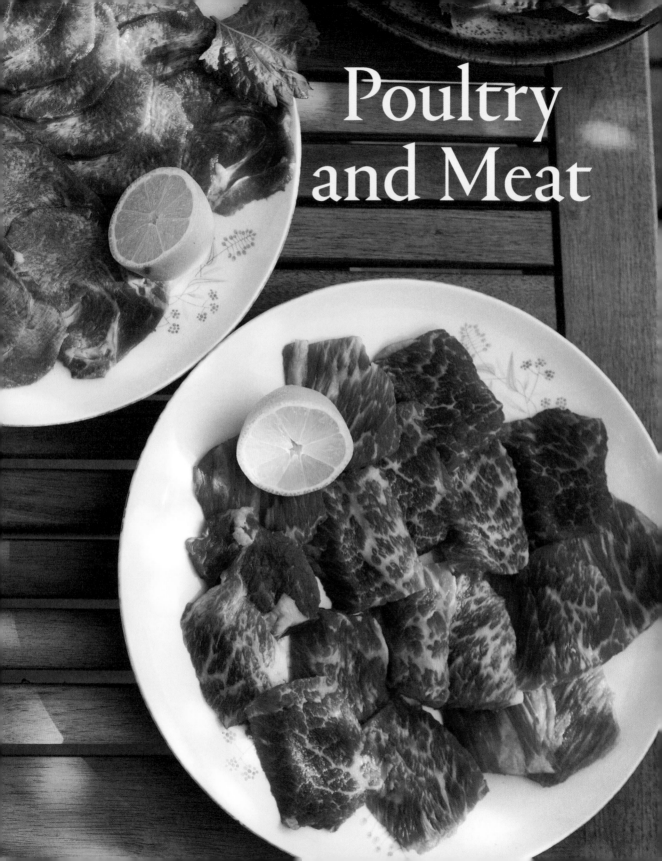

Poultry
and Meat

肉

In Japan, meat is celebrated, but the emphasis is on quality, not quantity. Part of this has to do with the geography of the country: Japan is small and mountainous, with limited grazing land, so the goal is not to raise a lot of cattle, but to make their meat as tasty as can be. That's why Japanese beef, called wagyu, is known for its exceptional quality. The accepted wisdom is that one should eat three times more vegetables than meat for a balanced diet. While many meals include meat as a component, it's not necessarily the main event. Perhaps because it's special, Japanese meat dishes tend to be so fine-tuned as to border on sublime.

If you've ever been to a yakitori restaurant, you may have tried tsukune, or chicken meatballs. They're moist and fluffy, shot through with bits of scallions, ginger, and garlic. To achieve that texture, you need to mix the ingredients thoroughly to get some air in. Using egg white instead of a whole egg helps make the meatballs softer and keeps them light. If using farm-fresh eggs, save the leftover raw yolks to use as a dipping sauce for the baked tsukune, a traditional way we eat them at home after they've been glazed in our teriyaki-like Kombu "Awesome Sauce" (page 35). We also like to dunk them in ponzu with grated daikon and shiso. Alternatively, you can use the raw tsukune mixture as a gyoza filling or drop it by the spoonful into a hotpot (page 149). It cooks fast—when the meatball floats up to the surface, it's done.

MAKES ABOUT 30 SMALL MEATBALLS (SERVES 4) • TOTAL TIME: 30 MINUTES

Preheat the oven to 450°F. Line a baking sheet with foil.

In a large bowl, combine the ground chicken, salt, soy sauce, sake, scallion whites, garlic, ginger, egg white, and a few cracks of black pepper. Mix vigorously by hand by making your hand into a claw shape and using it like a whisk for at least 2 minutes. (Wear a rubber or latex glove if you don't want your hands to get too messy.) The mixture should be almost sticky looking and very well blended. Add the cornstarch and blend well.

Prepare a small container filled with water, then dip a tablespoon into the water, scoop up a heaping spoonful of the tsukune mixture, and place it on the prepared baking sheet. (Since the mixture is very soft, you can't roll it into balls. If you want a rounder meatball, use a rounded tablespoon.) Repeat, dipping the spoon into the water between scoops so the mixture doesn't stick to the spoon. They will be round on top and flattened on the bottom, but that's okay. You should get about 30 tsukune. Brush with a bit of olive oil and bake until lightly golden and cooked through, 8 to 10 minutes. Serve immediately. Pour ponzu over the daikon in a small dish, and sprinkle some shiso on top. Eat with tsukune as a dipping sauce.

Note If you can only find ground chicken in 1-pound packages, we recommend buying 2 packs and freezing the leftover ½ pound to use the next time you make tsukune.

Tsukune

Chicken Meatballs

とりつくね

1½ pounds ground chicken, preferably dark meat, or a mix of dark and white meat (see Note)
2 teaspoons kosher salt
2 teaspoons soy sauce
2 teaspoons sake
8 scallions, white part only, halved lengthwise, then thinly sliced (about 1 cup)
2 garlic cloves, grated
2-inch piece of fresh ginger, peeled and finely grated
1 egg white
Freshly ground black pepper
2 tablespoons cornstarch
Olive oil, for brushing
½ cup ponzu sauce, homemade (page 36) or store-bought
About 1 cup finely grated daikon radish
4 to 6 shiso leaves, cut into thin ribbons

Variation:

GLAZED TSUKUNE:
When the tsukune are finished cooking, in a large skillet, bring 1 cup Kombu "Awesome Sauce" (page 35) to a boil over high heat. Lower the heat to medium and cook until the sauce thickens and reduces by about one-third, 3 to 4 minutes. Add the cooked tsukune, moving and turning them in the pan to glaze with the sauce, 1 to 2 minutes. Plate and serve with grated daikon and shiso.

Karaage

Japanese Fried Chicken

唐揚げ

2 pounds boneless, skin-on
  (if possible) chicken
  thighs (see Note),
  cut into quarters
3-inch piece of fresh ginger,
  peeled and grated
3 garlic cloves, grated
1 teaspoon sea salt, plus
  more for sprinkling
¼ cup sake
2 tablespoons soy sauce
1 large egg
Canola or other neutral oil,
  for deep-frying
¾ cup cornstarch or potato
  starch
¾ cup all-purpose flour
1 lemon, cut into wedges

Note If you can only find
bone-in, skin-on thighs and
would like to debone them:
(1) Place the meat skin-side
down on a cutting board.
Using the tip of a small,
sharp knife, slice along one
side of the bone, going no
deeper than the depth of
the bone. (2) Repeat on the
other side. The bone should
now be exposed. (3) Insert
the tip of the knife under the
middle of the bone with the
blade facing away from you.
Slice along the underside
of the bone, past the end of
the bone, detaching it from
the meat. (4) Rotate the thigh
180 degrees and repeat with
the other side of the bone to
detach it fully.

In Japan, you can find karaage everywhere, from high-end izakayas to convenience stores to the home kitchen. It's an everyday food, something you'd have for dinner, then put in a bento for lunch the next day. There are a few key things that make Japanese fried chicken extra special. First, it's made from the best part of the bird—dark meat—which gets marinated in an alchemical combination of ginger, garlic, soy sauce, and sake, making it extra succulent. The crust is lighter and crispier than others, thanks to the cornstarch in the breading, and the chicken is boneless, making it easy to devour in a couple of bites.

In Japan, fried chicken is also a Christmas food, thanks to a successful marketing campaign launched by Kentucky Fried Chicken in the 1970s, which linked the holiday to eating buckets of KFC. A typical Japanese Christmas meal might include fried chicken, Strawberry Shortcake (page 240), and a bottle of bubbly for adults, or sparkling juice for the kids. Instead of buying the fried chicken, my mom made it from scratch. This recipe is an adaptation of hers. —**Sawa**

SERVES 4 TO 6 • ACTIVE TIME: 1 HOUR • TOTAL TIME: 3 TO 12 HOURS, INCLUDING MARINATING

Place the quartered chicken thighs in a large bowl or a resealable plastic bag.

In a bowl, mix the ginger, garlic, salt, sake, soy sauce, and egg together until well blended. Transfer the marinade to the container with the chicken and mix to coat. Marinate, covered, in the refrigerator for at least 2 hours or up to overnight. The longer the chicken marinates, the more tender and flavorful it will be.

Line a baking sheet with two layers of paper towel. Pour 2 inches canola oil into a Dutch oven and heat over medium high heat to 350°F on a deep-fry thermometer.

Drain the chicken in a colander to get rid of excess liquid. In a shallow bowl, whisk the cornstarch with the flour. Dredge 4 or 5 pieces of chicken at a time, dusting off any excess. Using dry, heatproof tongs or wooden chopsticks, place the dredged chicken carefully into the hot oil, taking care not to splash.

Fry 4 or 5 pieces at a time (depending on the size of the pot) without overcrowding. Turn after 3 minutes and cook for 3 minutes more. The color should be a nice and golden brown. Transfer to the paper towels and sprinkle with salt. Serve with lemon wedges.

We love combining umami-rich miso with sticky honey in this simple, satisfying sheet-pan chicken dinner. It's our perfect weeknight meal. Both ingredients tenderize the meat, and when the juices from the chicken mix with the butter, miso, and honey, you get a delicious sauce right in the pan.

Our favorite style of chicken parts—boneless and skin-on—is the best of both worlds: the convenience of boneless chicken, with the succulence from the skin. If you can't find it in stores, buy bone-in pieces and ask a butcher to debone them for you. Or just use our favorite part of the bird, the thighs, and do it yourself (see Note, page 188). While we prefer the skin on, boneless, skinless chicken works, too, as do bone-in parts, though they'll take 2 to 3 minutes longer to cook.

SERVES 4 • ACTIVE TIME: 30 MINUTES • TOTAL TIME: 2½ TO 24 HOURS, DEPENDING ON HOW LONG YOU MARINATE THE CHICKEN

Miso-Honey Broiled Chicken

チキンのはちみつ味噌焼き

2 pounds boneless, skin-on chicken thighs or breasts, or a mix of both
6 tablespoons aka (red) or awase (blended) miso
3 tablespoons honey
4 scallions, halved
1 tablespoon cold unsalted butter, cut into ⅛-inch-thick slices
4 lemon wedges

Put the chicken pieces in a container or a resealable plastic bag and evenly spread the miso and honey over all of it. Refrigerate for at least 2 hours or up to overnight. Don't go longer than 24 hours or the chicken will start to dry out.

Position a rack 6 inches from the broiler element and set the broiler to high.

Line a sheet pan with foil. Place the scallions in an even layer to create a bed to rest the chicken on. Lay the chicken on the scallions, skin-side up, placing them close together without touching. Scoop up the excess marinade and put it between the chicken and the scallions to help make a sauce as it cooks. Distribute the pieces of butter evenly over the chicken thighs.

Broil the chicken until the skin starts to get crispy and the honey and miso caramelize to a golden brown, about 6 minutes. Some parts might get a little black, which is expected with the honey. (Just be careful not to char it too much.)

Turn off the broiler and set the oven to 400°F. Continue cooking until the chicken is just cooked through, another 7 to 9 minutes. (It's okay if your oven takes time to get to 400°F; the point is to lower the temperature so that the chicken cooks through.) To test if the chicken is done, insert a cake tester or the tip of a small knife into the thickest part of the thigh, then feel how warm it is. If it borders on hot, the chicken is cooked. If not, continue to cook for another 2 to 3 minutes, and check again for doneness.

Remove the chicken from the oven and let it rest for 5 minutes. (The chicken will continue to cook from residual heat.) Transfer the chicken and scallions to a serving platter and spoon over any sauce that is left on the sheet pan. Serve immediately with lemon wedges on the side.

Oyakodon

Chicken and Egg over Rice

親子丼

1 pound boneless chicken
    thighs, cut into 1-inch
    cubes
4 tablespoons sake
1 teaspoon kosher salt
6 cups cooked Japanese
    white or multigrain rice
    (page 215)
3 tablespoons mirin
2 tablespoons soy sauce
½ cup Dashi (page 33) or
    ½ teaspoon dashi powder
    mixed into ½ cup water
1 yellow onion, thinly sliced
1 cup sliced shiitake
    mushroom caps
    (optional)
1 teaspoon minced fresh
    ginger
2 eggs, lightly beaten
2 scallions, thinly sliced,
    or 8 sprigs of mitsuba,
    roughly chopped or torn

The main ingredients in oyakodon are chicken and egg, so appropriately, the name means "parent and child." It's a brothy, light stew, laced with tender bites of chicken, sweet onion, and custardy eggs cooked in dashi. There's rice in this recipe because any dish with "don" in its name is served over rice.

Just-set eggs are the key to great oyakodon. You want them soft but not runny. To get it right, start by not overbeating the eggs. Then make sure the stew is bubbling at a gentle simmer before pouring them in. Rather than dumping in the eggs at once, I use a pair of cooking chopsticks to reduce the flow to a drizzle, and pour in a circular motion for even distribution. Then, I gently shake the pan, remove from the heat, and put the lid on. Serve the eggs when they have just set, or right before, to prevent overcooking. When I'm eating, I like to mix it all together with the rice so I can get everything in one bite.

I prefer using chicken thighs, but the recipe works with breasts, too (though you might want to cook them a minute or two less). If you have it, in place of scallions, consider sprinkling the oyakodon with mitsuba, a refreshing herb that combines beautifully with dashi. —**Sawa**

SERVES 4 • TOTAL TIME: 40 MINUTES

In a bowl or container, combine the chicken with 1 tablespoon of the sake and the salt, and mix to coat. Cover and marinate in the refrigerator for a few hours, or for a few minutes if you don't have the time.

Make the rice as directed.

In a large skillet or a shallow braiser with a lid, combine the remaining 3 tablespoons sake, the mirin, soy sauce, and dashi and bring to a boil over medium heat. Add the onion and shiitake, reduce the heat to medium-low, cover, and simmer until the onions are translucent, about 5 minutes.

Add the ginger and the marinated chicken and simmer gently, covered, until the chicken is opaque and just cooked through, about 7 minutes. You can cut a piece open or insert a cake tester to check for doneness (if it is cooked through, the cake tester will be hot to the touch). Remove the lid, increase the heat to high, and pour in the eggs, taking care to disperse them evenly around the entire pan. Do not stir. Once the eggs and sauce start to bubble, which should happen quickly, put the lid back on and remove from the heat. Let stand for 2 minutes.

While the dish is resting, scoop the warm rice into four bowls.

Remove the lid. The eggs should be soft, but set. Divide evenly among the bowls, scooping the eggs and sauce over the rice. Sprinkle with the scallions and serve immediately.

Tonkatsu, a juicy pork cutlet with a craggy fried panko crust, is an iconic dish with broad appeal. Here we serve it the most classic way, with tonkatsu sauce (also known as katsu sauce), shredded cabbage, and a squeeze of lemon. But there are so many variations: You can eat it with curry ladled on top (katsu curry), in a sando (katsu sando), in a bento box for katsu-ben, or sliced and cooked again in dashi and egg over rice (katsu-don), similar to Oyakodon on the opposite page. When my mom would cook us tonkatsu for dinner, she always made extras to put in my bento the next morning, or to freeze for katsu-don for a future lunch.

Tonkatsu is usually deep-fried, but we pan-fry ours and baste it with butter, herbs, and garlic to give it even more flavor. If you can find it, use good-quality pork from a Berkshire pig or another heritage breed. **—Sawa**

SERVES 4 • TOTAL TIME: 1 HOUR

To make the tonkatsu sauce: In a small bowl, mix together the okonomi sauce and vinegar. Transfer to a serving bowl and set aside. Tonkatsu sauce can be made ahead and stored covered in the refrigerator for up to 1 year.

To prepare the cutlets: Put a pork chop on a cutting board. Place a piece of plastic wrap over the pork chop and use a meat mallet to pound it to about ½ inch thick. Repeat with the remaining pork chops.

Season each pork chop with ½ teaspoon of the salt and a few cracks of black pepper.

Set up a breading station: Set up three shallow bowls large enough to hold a single pork chop, with a bit of room to spare. Put the flour in the first, the eggs in the second, and the panko and lemon zest in the third. At the end of the line have a dish large enough to hold all 4 cutlets.

Dredge a pork chop in flour, coating both sides and dusting off any excess. Using a fork, dip it into the eggs, coating both sides thoroughly. Transfer to the panko mixture and coat generously on both sides. Transfer the breaded cutlet to the large dish and repeat with the remaining pork chops.

Line a baking sheet with two layers of paper towel and have at the ready.

continued

Tonkatsu

Fried Pork Cutlet

トンカツ

Tonkatsu Sauce

1 cup okonomi sauce, homemade (page 34) or store-bought, such as Otafuku brand

1 teaspoon rice vinegar

Cutlets

4 boneless pork chops, 1 inch thick (6 to 8 ounces each)

2 teaspoons kosher salt, plus more for seasoning

Freshly ground black pepper

1 cup all-purpose flour

2 eggs, lightly beaten

2 cups panko bread crumbs

1 lemon, zested and cut into quarters

Canola oil or other neutral oil, for frying

4 tablespoons unsalted butter

4 sprigs of thyme or rosemary (optional)

4 garlic cloves (optional), peeled but whole

4 cups shredded green cabbage

In a large skillet, preferably cast-iron, heat ¼ inch canola oil over medium heat. When the oil starts to shimmer, carefully lay a cutlet in the oil. It should be sizzling gently. Cook until the bottom of the cutlet just starts to turn golden brown, 2 to 3 minutes. Flip and add 1 tablespoon of the butter, 1 sprig of thyme, and a garlic clove. Cook until the second side turns a deep golden brown, 3 to 4 minutes. Flip the cutlet again, cooking until the first side turns a deep golden brown, 1 to 2 minutes longer. Transfer to the baking sheet lined with paper towels. Season each side with a pinch of salt. Discard the oil from the pan and repeat with the remaining cutlets, fresh oil, butter, thyme, and garlic.

To serve, divide the shredded cabbage among four plates, place a cutlet next to each mound of cabbage, and garnish with a lemon wedge. Serve with the tonkatsu sauce on the side.

Tonjiru literally means "pork soup," but it's so much more than that. It has all the comfort of miso soup, but with the addition of pork and lots of vegetables; it's more substantial and hearty. I like to put in a lot of vegetables and make a big pot of it in the wintertime. I eat this with rice as a simple lunch, or serve a smaller amount to accompany rice and a main dish for dinner. If you can't find burdock, then another root vegetable such as potato, rutabaga, or turnip would work as well. If you don't have saikyo shiro miso, which is the sweetest type of miso, you can make this dish with most other kinds, with the exception of the extra-dark hatcho miso. **—Sawa**

SERVES 4 TO 6 • TOTAL TIME: 30 MINUTES

Put the konnyaku in a small pot and massage a few pinches of salt into it. Pour in enough water to cover and bring to a boil over high heat. Boil for 2 minutes, drain, and let cool to room temperature.

In a pot, heat the oil over medium heat. Add the pork and ginger and cook, stirring every few minutes, until the fat is rendered and the pork starts to brown, 4 to 6 minutes.

Add the sake and stir. Cook until the sake is reduced by half, 30 seconds to 1 minute.

Add the konnyaku, dashi, carrots, daikon, gobo, and scallions. Increase the heat to high and bring to a boil. Reduce the heat to a gentle simmer and skim any foam or impurities off the top of the soup. Cook until the carrots and daikon are tender but not mushy, 15 to 20 minutes.

Put the miso into a small bowl. Ladle about ½ cup of the liquid from the soup over the miso and stir together to make a wet paste. Pour the miso mixture into the soup and stir to dissolve the miso completely. Taste and season with a little more salt if you wish, then ladle the soup into serving bowls. Sprinkle the mitsuba over each bowl of soup and serve hot.

Tonjiru

Hearty Pork Miso Soup

豚汁

⅔ cup tama konnyaku (balls), halved, or 1 (3-ounce) brick konnyaku, cut into pieces the size of a postage stamp

Kosher salt or fine sea salt

2 teaspoons canola oil or other neutral oil

8 ounces pork belly or pork shoulder, thinly sliced and cut into pieces the size of a postage stamp

1-inch piece of fresh ginger, peeled and julienned

¼ cup sake

8 cups Dashi (page 33) or 2 tablespoons plus 2 teaspoons dashi powder mixed into 8 cups water

6 ounces carrots, halved lengthwise, then sliced crosswise on the diagonal into slices ⅛ inch thick

6 ounces daikon radish, peeled and cut into tanzaku (see page 31)

4 ounces gobo (burdock root), scrubbed clean, cut on the diagonal into slices ⅛ inch thick

6 scallions, white part only, cut into ½-inch lengths

Heaping ⅓ cup saikyo shiro (white) miso

8 sprigs mitsuba or parsley, leaves torn and stems cut small for garnish

Pork Chops
with Teriyaki-Bacon Jam

ポークステーキの
ベーコンジャム添え

6 ounces slab bacon,
    cut into ¼-inch dice
1 large yellow onion,
    thinly sliced
2 tablespoons mirin
2 tablespoons sugar
3 tablespoons soy sauce
2 teaspoons rice vinegar
2 large bone-in pork chops,
    1 inch thick (about 1 pound
    each)
1 tablespoon canola oil or
    other neutral oil
Salt and freshly ground
    black pepper

We love pork chops in our house, and topping them with a sweet, smoky bacon jam makes them irresistible. It's a sauce and a condiment in one, as fantastic slathered on a burger as it is on a turkey sandwich, or drizzled over vegetables and rice. Though we prefer bone-in pork chops, this preparation can work with any cut of pork that cooks well in a skillet. Boneless pork chops, pork loin, or tenderloin are all fine substitutes, but you may have to adjust the cooking time depending on the cut. We like to serve this dish with a big bowl salad, such as our Kale Salad with Carrot-Ginger Dressing (page 63).

SERVES 4 • TOTAL TIME: 1 HOUR

In a pot, cook the bacon over medium heat, stirring occasionally, until the bacon just starts to brown but is not yet crispy and the fat is mostly melted, 5 to 7 minutes. Add the onion, reduce the heat to medium-low, and cook until the onions are soft and translucent, 10 to 15 minutes, taking care to stir every few minutes.

Add the mirin, sugar, and soy sauce and cook until the liquid has reduced to a syrupy, marmalade-like consistency, 10 to 15 minutes. Stir in the vinegar and set aside.

Preheat the oven to 350°F. Set a cooling rack in a sheet pan and set aside.

Heat a large ovenproof grill pan or cast-iron skillet over high heat. Rub the pork chops with the oil and season each side generously with salt and pepper. If using a grill pan, place the pork chops in the pan, cook for 3 minutes, then rotate 90 degrees and cook for another 3 minutes to create crosshatch marks. Flip and repeat on the other side. If using a cast-iron skillet, cook until golden and caramelized, about 6 minutes on the first side, then repeat on the other side.

Transfer the pan to the oven and finish cooking the pork chops for 3 to 4 minutes for medium doneness, flipping over halfway through the cooking time.

Remove the pork chops from the oven and transfer to the cooling rack to rest for 5 to 7 minutes. This lets the juices settle and ensures the pork chop will be moist when you cut it. If the bacon jam is cool at this stage, warm it up over medium heat before serving.

Transfer the pork chops to a cutting board and remove the bone. Slice crosswise into pieces about ½ inch thick. Transfer to a serving platter, spoon a few tablespoons of the bacon jam on top (or as much as you like) and serve immediately. Store leftover bacon jam in the refrigerator for up to 1 week, or freeze for up to 3 months.

Hambagu

ハンバーグ

1 slice white bread, torn into
    small pieces
½ cup milk
2 tablespoons vegetable oil,
    plus more for frying
1 yellow onion, finely diced
1 carrot, finely diced
4 celery stalks, finely diced
1 sprig of thyme
1 garlic clove, grated
1 zucchini (about 8 ounces),
    grated on the small holes
    of a box grater, water
    squeezed out
1 egg
6 ounces soft tofu, water
    squeezed out
½ cup grated Parmigiano-
    Reggiano cheese
2½ teaspoons salt
½ teaspoon freshly ground
    black pepper
¼ teaspoon freshly grated
    nutmeg
1 pound ground beef
1 pound ground pork
½ cup okonomi sauce,
    homemade (page 34),
    or store-bought, such as
    Otafuku brand

Hambagu is basically meatloaf in a patty form. Every mom in Japan has her own recipe—it's that popular. I like adding veggies and tofu so it's healthier. The kids love it, and they don't even know there are vegetables in there! This recipe makes enough to feed a family of four for two meals. You can cook half of the batch, freeze the rest raw, then put them in the refrigerator to thaw the morning before you plan on cooking them—you'll be happy you did when you don't feel like making dinner from scratch. Or, cook them all and use up leftovers in a Hambagu Melt (page 116) or pack cold in a bento box (see Bento Boxes, page 109).

When squeezing water from zucchini and tofu, be thorough. I like to put them in a paper towel and wring them out a little bit at a time until no more water drips out. If you feel the mixture is too wet, you can always add a bit of panko or other bread crumbs to soak up the excess moisture. The recipe will also work if you wish to use all beef or ground poultry. —**Sawa**

SERVES 6 TO 8 • TOTAL TIME: 1 HOUR 15 MINUTES

In a small bowl, soak the torn bread in the milk.

Heat a large skillet over medium-high heat. Add the oil and onion and cook for a few minutes, until it's fragrant but hasn't taken on any color. Add the carrot, celery, and thyme and cook, stirring frequently, for about 5 minutes. When the onions start to turn translucent, reduce the heat to low and cook, stirring occasionally, until the vegetables are soft and have melded together, like a sofrito, about 10 minutes. Add the garlic, stir, and remove from the heat. Transfer to a large bowl and let cool to room temperature. Discard the thyme stem.

Add the zucchini, egg, tofu, and the milk-soaked bread (discarding excess milk if there is any) to the cooled vegetables. Add the Parmigiano-Reggiano, salt, pepper, nutmeg, and ground meat. Mix by hand (remove your rings!) until well combined.

To shape the patties, divide the mixture into 16 equal balls. Slightly flatten each into a disk roughly 2½ inches wide and ¾ inch thick. Make a small indentation in the center of the patty—when you cook it, the center will puff up. If you wish to freeze them, place on a parchment-lined baking sheet, spaced slightly apart, and put in the freezer. Once the patties are firm, transfer to a resealable bag and keep frozen for up to 2 months.

In a large heavy skillet, such as cast-iron, heat 1 tablespoon vegetable oil over medium-high heat. Place the patties in the pan, indented-side up, fitting as many as you can without crowding. The patties should not be touching. Cook until browned and caramelized on the outside and firm to the touch, about 5 minutes on each side. Remove and put on a serving platter. Repeat with the remaining patties.

Add the okonomi sauce to the drippings in the pan you used to fry the hambagu. (If freezing half the patties, only add half the okonomi sauce. Refrigerate the rest to use when you cook the second batch.) Warm over medium heat, stirring and deglazing the pan of some of the caramelized bits, for about a minute. The sauce should be the consistency of ketchup. If it's too thick, add a teaspoon or two of water to thin it out and cook until you've achieved the desired consistency.

Spoon the sauce over the patties and serve with your favorite sides.

As someone who grew up in an Ashkenazi Jewish household, I have a real soft spot for stuffed cabbage. When Sawa told me that she grew up eating it, too, I was intrigued. It turns out it's also a staple of Japanese home cooking, another example of yoshoku (dishes of foreign origin adapted to Japanese cuisine). I was curious to see how it would be adapted to Japanese tastes. The ground meat and rice filling is familiar, but the broth sets it apart. Braising the cabbage rolls in dashi gives the dish a lightness that you just don't get with a tomato-based sauce. But we do get that all-important sweet and sour flavor with a generous dollop of ketchup. Don't laugh—wait until you try it. **—Aaron**

SERVES 4 • TOTAL TIME: 1 HOUR

Bring a large pot of water to a boil. Line a baking sheet with paper towels.

Using a small, sharp knife, cut the core out of the cabbage. Carefully lower the cabbage into the boiling water. After about a minute, the outer leaves should be soft enough to gently peel off with tongs. Transfer the leaves to the prepared baking sheet. Continue peeling off the outer leaves as they soften and cook, until you have 8 large leaves. (If some look small, you might want a few extra.) Remove the cabbage from the pot and save for another use, such as Hiroshima-Style Okonomiyaki (page 81).

Place a cabbage leaf flat on a cutting board, rib-side up. Using a small knife, shave down the thick part of the rib by about half so it will be easier to roll. Repeat with the remaining leaves.

In a large skillet, heat the olive oil over medium-low heat. Add the onion and cook, stirring occasionally, until it starts to soften, 2 to 3 minutes. Add the mushrooms, garlic, and ginger and continue cooking, stirring occasionally to avoid browning, until the onions are soft and translucent, the mushrooms are cooked through, and there is no liquid in the pan, 7 to 8 minutes. Remove from the heat and set aside to cool to room temperature.

In a large bowl, combine the ground beef, pork, and rice. Add the onion mixture, 2 teaspoons of the salt, several cracks of black pepper, and about 10 strokes of nutmeg grated on a Microplane. Using your hands, thoroughly mix the filling until combined. Divide into 8 equal portions in the bowl.

continued

Rolled Cabbage in Dashi

ロールキャベツ

1 head green cabbage
1 tablespoon olive oil
1 small yellow onion, finely diced (about 1 cup)
6 to 7 shiitake mushroom caps, finely diced (about 1 cup)
1 garlic clove, minced
1 teaspoon minced fresh ginger
8 ounces ground beef
8 ounces ground pork
1 cup cooked rice (preferably Japanese White Rice, page 215)
4 teaspoons kosher salt
Freshly ground black pepper
Freshly grated nutmeg
2 cups Dashi (page 33) or 2 teaspoons dashi powder mixed into 2 cups water
2 tablespoons sake
1 bay leaf
Ketchup, for serving

To stuff the cabbage, lay a leaf on a cutting board with the part that attaches to the core closest to you. Place a portion of filling horizontally in the center of the leaf and pat to shape into a cylinder. Fold the side of the leaf closest to you over the filling, fold the sides toward the center, then roll until the filling is fully enclosed in the cabbage leaf. Place, seam-side down, in a large braiser with a lid. Repeat with the remaining filling and cabbage leaves until you have 8 rolls arranged in a single layer in the pan.

Pour the dashi and sake over the cabbage rolls, then add the bay leaf and the remaining 2 teaspoons salt. Set over high heat and bring to a boil. Reduce the heat to low, cover, and cook at a low simmer until the cabbage leaves are tender enough to cut with a spoon, 15 to 20 minutes (at this point, the meat will be cooked through). If you like your cabbage even softer, cook for up to 30 minutes. Serve while piping hot, with ketchup.

Note If you have raw Hambagu (page 200) in your freezer, it's a great filling for rolled cabbage. Just thaw the raw patties before using—use 1 per cabbage roll (or about half the hambagu recipe for this amount of cabbage).

People say that this dish was introduced to Japanese cooks in the Imperial Navy in the late 1800s, after an admiral developed a taste for beef stew in England. Although nikujaga has its roots in Western cuisine, it has since become ubiquitous in Japan, eaten in the cooler months over a bowl of steaming white rice. My mom used to make it for our family in the winter. Because of how easy it is to find most of the ingredients for it in the US, it was one of the first things I cooked for myself when I was a college student in Texas.

This is less of a beef stew than it is a vegetable braise with some meat for flavor. We use the same thinly sliced beef that we buy at the Japanese grocer for hotpot (see Buying and Slicing Meat, page 148), but you can just cut some meat as thin as you can and pound it with a meat mallet or the back of a pot to get it even thinner. When making nikujaga, it's important to keep the lid on when simmering to prevent evaporation and drying out, since not much liquid is added. A heavy pot with a lid that has a good seal, like a braiser from Le Creuset or Staub, is ideal for this dish.

Nikujaga is really about the potatoes, so go out of your way to get good ones. We like potatoes from the farmers' market, as they're always more flavorful and creamier than what we find at the grocery store. The potatoes are always better the next day after soaking up all the flavors. —**Sawa**

SERVES 4 • TOTAL TIME: 45 MINUTES

Nikujaga

Beef and Potato Stew

肉じゃが

8 ounces konnyaku noodles or shirataki

1 tablespoon toasted sesame oil

8 ounces thinly sliced beef (sirloin, rib eye, or chuck roll)

1½ pounds small Yukon Gold or German Butterball potatoes (the size of golf balls), peeled and halved, or quartered if larger

2 cups 1-inch chunks peeled carrots

1 large yellow onion, halved through the root, then cut into ½-inch slices

½ cup sake

3 tablespoons sugar

4½ tablespoons soy sauce

Cooked Japanese White Rice (page 215), for serving

Bring a small pot of water to a boil over high heat. Add the konnyaku noodles and boil for 2 minutes. Drain and set aside.

In a 3- to 4-quart saucepot with a tight-fitting lid pot, or a braiser, heat the sesame oil over medium-high heat. When the oil is shimmering, add the beef and cook, stirring frequently, until lightly browned, about 5 minutes. Using cooking chopsticks or a spoon, remove the beef from the pot, leaving the oil behind, and place the beef in a bowl.

To the braiser, add the potatoes, carrots, onion, and konnyaku noodles and cook, stirring frequently, until the onions just start to turn translucent, 3 to 4 minutes. Add the sake, sugar, and soy sauce and bring to a boil. Lower the heat to a gentle simmer, return the meat to the pot, cover, and cook for 10 minutes. Uncover and gently stir the stew, taking care to carefully turn over the potatoes. Put the lid back on and cook until the tip of a knife or cake tester can be easily inserted into the potatoes, 10 to 15 minutes. Remove from the heat and serve with white rice. Store, covered, in the refrigerator for up to 4 days.

Japanese Curry

カレーライス

2 tablespoons olive oil
1 tablespoon unsalted butter
1 large onion, thinly sliced
1 pound beef stew meat,
    pork shoulder, or
    boneless chicken thighs,
    cut into bite-size cubes
1 teaspoon kosher salt,
    plus more to taste
2 teaspoons curry powder
2 garlic cloves, minced
1 tablespoon minced
    fresh ginger
3 Yukon Gold potatoes,
    peeled and cut into
    bite-size chunks
1 large carrot, peeled and
    cut into bite-size pieces
4 Hakurei turnips, tops
    removed, cleaned and
    cut into bite-size pieces
1 quart water
4 ounces curry sauce mix,
    chopped into small
    pieces
½ apple, peeled and grated
1 teaspoon awase (blended)
    or aka (red) miso
1 square of dark chocolate
1 teaspoon soy sauce
1 teaspoon Worcestershire
    sauce
Japanese White Rice
    (page 215) or yellow rice
    (see Note)
Grated Cheddar cheese
    (optional)
Rakkyo Pickles (page 209)

When I was in high school in Hiroshima, I worked as a waitress at a curry restaurant. Staff meal was always curry, a thick brown gravy with all kinds of spices in it, a meat of your choice, and root vegetables, served over yellow turmeric rice. I looked forward to eating it every time I worked a shift—I loved watching the chef make the delicious-looking plates. He said the recipe was top secret, and I never did find out what went into his curry.

Over the years, I've developed my own recipe. I caramelize an onion to a deep brown, which enhances the flavor tenfold. I add other unconventional ingredients, like grated apple, miso, chocolate, soy sauce, and Worcestershire sauce, to give the gravy a sweet-savory complexity. I use S&B curry mix, a condensed curry roux, which you can purchase at most Asian markets. It thickens the stew and is an instant umami bomb. I suspect it's not super healthy, but it's what I grew up eating and it's what I crave. Sometimes I sprinkle grated sharp Cheddar over the rice before spooning the curry on top for a nice, melty layer, a trick I learned from the restaurant.

I like to serve mine with Rakkyo Pickles (page 209). A type of allium, rakkyo are similar to ramps, and the pickles provide a dynamic crunch and sweetness that goes amazingly well with the curry. **—Sawa**

SERVES 4 TO 6 • ACTIVE TIME: 30 MINUTES • TOTAL TIME: 1 HOUR 45 MINUTES

Preheat the oven to 475°F. Line a sheet pan with foil.

Heat a large braiser, such as Le Creuset or Staub, or a 4-quart saucepot with a tight-fitting lid over medium heat. Add 1 tablespoon of the olive oil, the butter, and onion, stirring frequently. Once they start to sizzle, reduce the heat to low and cook, stirring frequently, until the onions take on a deep golden caramelized color, 15 to 20 minutes. If the onions start to burn or stick to the pan, add a splash or two of water and scrape to deglaze it.

Meanwhile, in a bowl, toss the meat with the remaining 1 tablespoon olive oil, the salt, and curry powder. Spread onto the prepared pan in an even layer and roast until the meat has browned a little, 8 to 10 minutes. Remove the roasted meat and set aside until the onions are caramelized.

Once the onions in the braiser have caramelized, stir in the garlic and ginger and cook until aromatic, about 1 minute. Add the roasted meat, potatoes, carrot, turnips, and 1 quart water. Increase the heat to high, bring to a boil,

continued

then reduce the heat to low. Skim any foam and fat that comes to the surface, cover, and simmer, stirring occasionally to prevent it from sticking to the bottom of the pot, until the meat and vegetables are tender but not mushy, 1 hour to 1 hour 15 minutes (or 45 minutes to 1 hour for chicken). The curry should be gently bubbling the whole time.

Remove from the heat, then stir in the curry sauce mix, grated apple, miso, chocolate, soy sauce, and Worcestershire sauce until fully incorporated. The curry should have a gravy-like consistency. Warm the curry over medium heat. Taste for seasoning, adding more salt if needed. Serve over rice (if using Cheddar, sprinkle a small handful over the rice before ladling the curry on top), with rakkyo pickles on the side.

Note To make yellow rice, stir 1½ teaspoons ground turmeric into the Japanese White Rice (page 215) before cooking.

When I first met Sawa, she had this tiny mini fridge in her apartment. Tucked in the back was a container of her mother's rakkyo pickles, which were shipped from Japan. Like other fukujinzuke (pickles that are eaten with curry), they provide a sweet, acidic, crunchy counterpoint to the spicy stew. Rakkyo is an allium with a small bulb and slightly garlicky flavor. They're difficult to find in the US, but Suzuki Farm in Delaware grows them and ships within the region. The next best thing are ramps, which we forage in the spring, but pearl onions or very small shallots are also good substitutes. If this quantity is too much, the recipe can easily be scaled down. **—Aaron**

MAKES 2 QUARTS • ACTIVE TIME: 30 MINUTES • TOTAL TIME: ABOUT 3 WEEKS

Rakkyo Pickles

らっきょう漬け

2 pounds rakkyo, ramps, pearl onions, or very small shallots
1 cup kosher salt
1½ cups rice vinegar
¾ cup mirin
¾ cup sugar
1 dried togarashi chile or a pinch of chile flakes

If using rakkyo or ramps, trim the roots off the bulbs, and cut off the tops about 1 inch above the bulb. Reserve the tops for another use (rakkyo tops are fibrous and tough to eat, but make a great stock; ramp tops have many uses, from sautés to pesto). Peel off the outer layer of the bulb if it's dirty or dry. If using pearl onions or shallots, trim the roots and peel them.

Bring a large pot of water to a boil.

Sterilize a 2-quart glass jar and lid by submerging them in the boiling water for a minute (the lid should not be screwed onto the jar). Let cool and air-dry. Add the rakkyo and salt to the jar. Cover with enough water to fully submerge and place a weight, such as a small ramekin or plate, on the rakkyo to keep them under the surface. Cover with a small piece of plastic wrap and the lid and let it sit at room temperature for 4 days.

Drain the rakkyo, then rinse with cold water in a bowl. Drain and set aside.

In a small pot, bring the vinegar, mirin, and sugar to a boil. Let boil for 1 minute, then remove from the heat and let cool to room temperature.

Sterilize the jar the same way as before, then let cool and air-dry. Put the drained rakkyo in the jar. Add the dried togarashi chile and pour in the pickling liquid so that it covers the rakkyo (they may float a little). Keep the rakkyo submerged with the weight, and cover with a small piece of plastic wrap and the lid. Store in a cool spot, such as the back of a kitchen cupboard or pantry, for 3 weeks before eating. When it's ready, the pickles will be crunchy and have a sweet, pungent smell. Refrigerate after opening. They will keep in the refrigerator for at least a year. Serve with curry, or anywhere a sweet garlicky pickle is good.

BATHING AND BLACK BEAN TEA

Bathing is an integral part of Japanese culture. Three-quarters of Japan's land is mountainous, and there are quite a few volcanoes, too. This unique combination of geological conditions creates onsen, or hot springs, mineral-rich water that is good for healing your mind and body.

Most Japanese people soak in a tub every day, either at home, in a local bathhouse, or by taking a special trip to an onsen ryokan, a traditional inn where you go to relax, bathe in the hot springs, eat great food, sleep it off, and repeat. Of course, when Aaron came to Japan with me for the first time, I had to take him to one.

We were in my dad's car, driving to the onsen ryokan he had booked, and I was trying to explain the bath culture to Aaron. I could tell he was nervous and wanted to hide it from my parents. (He was willing, but a bit uncomfortable, to get naked in front of strangers, especially his future father-in-law.) My mom, a gentle soul, looked at me from the passenger seat and said, "Don't worry Aaron-san, oto-san (meaning my father) can't see anything once he takes his glasses off."

We had a good laugh. Whether it reassured Aaron or not, he did go into the onsen with my dad. When he was going through the noren (curtain partition) and looked back at me waving and smiling at him for encouragement, he smiled back, and disappeared into the men's area. All it took was one soak in the hinoki tub, and he more or less shed his inhibitions and became a fan for life.

Afterwards, we sat in the communal resting area and drank cold tea from a big dispenser. It was black bean tea—nutty, savory, a touch sweet, refreshing and rejuvenating all at once. Our body heat was high from the bath. We sipped the tea and sat there for a while. It was so calm in the room, just me and Aaron in yukata (a cotton kimono). That moment stayed with us.

Since then, we brew black bean tea at home, and buy bath powder from the Japanese grocery store, such as Bath Roman or Tabino Yado brands, which re-creates the aromas and minerality of the onsen. After a long day of standing in the restaurant kitchen, we soak in the tub, have a glass of iced black bean tea, and think back to that relaxing day. —**Sawa**

Rice

ご飯もの

Rice is so important that *gohan*, the word meaning "cooked rice," is also the word for "food," so learning to cook Japanese food well inevitably depends on understanding rice. Although a bowl of steaming rice accompanies most home-cooked meals, when served as part of a formal multicourse kaiseki, it comes as a final dish, before the sweets. That's because filling up on rice before that point will dampen your appetite for sake (the idea being that when you're hungry, you'll drink more). The same reasoning extends to izakayas, where to cap off a night of drinking, people will order a rice dish or another heavy starch and call it *shime*, or "finish."

Rice is the easiest thing to make if you have a rice cooker, because all you have to do is press a button for perfectly cooked rice. We love our Zojirushi for this reason. If you don't have a rice cooker, what follows is a simple stovetop method that's pretty much foolproof. We get the best results when using a heavy enamel-coated cast-iron pot, such as a Staub or Le Creuset. A donabe pot works well, too. Both types distribute heat evenly and keep in as much steam as possible, which is ideal for making rice. Steam retention is also why it's crucial to cook the rice without opening the lid. To check if it's boiling, listen for bubbling sounds, and look for steam starting to hiss out the sides.

Leftover rice freezes well in an airtight container or wrapped in plastic. Reheat in the microwave for 2 minutes directly from the freezer, and it's almost as good as when you cooked it.

MAKES 6 CUPS (SERVES 4 TO 6 AS AN ACCOMPANIMENT TO A MEAL) • TOTAL TIME: 30 MINUTES

Japanese White Rice

Gohan

ご飯

2¼ cups (3 rice-cooker cups, see Note) Japanese white rice, washed and drained (see Washing Rice, page 216)
2½ cups water (if cooking on the stovetop)

If cooking on the stovetop: Put the washed rice into a heavy-duty medium pot with a tight-fitting lid, such as an enameled cast-iron pot like Staub or Le Creuset. Add the 2½ cups water, cover, and bring to a boil over high heat, 6 to 9 minutes. Do not open the lid—instead, to check if it's boiling, look for steam and listen for bubbling sounds. Immediately reduce the heat to low and cook for exactly 10 minutes. Remove from the heat. Let sit, covered, for 10 minutes.

If using a rice cooker: Put the washed rice in the bowl of a rice cooker. Add enough water to reach the 3-cup line for white rice. Cook on the "white rice" setting.

When the rice is finished cooking, carefully open the lid. Dip a rice paddle in water to prevent the grains from sticking to it. Fluff the rice by scooping down to the bottom and gently folding up a few times. Some steam will be released and the rice will be more aerated.

Scoop the rice into four or six bowls, depending on how many people you are serving.

Note If you have a rice cooker, the measuring cup that comes with it is a Japanese rice cup, which is smaller than a standard American cup. (A Japanese rice cup is 180 milliliters, or ¾ of an American cup.) We adjusted the measurement of the rice to reflect standard American cup sizes in case you are making the recipe on the stovetop, and offer the Japanese rice cup measurements if you are using a rice cooker.

Variation

MULTIGRAIN RICE (pictured on pages 212–213): Substitute ¼ cup multigrain rice for ¼ cup of the white rice, add 2 more tablespoons of water. The multigrain rice will have a nice rosy color from the different grains, as well as nutty flavor and a varied texture. Eat anytime you would eat white rice, except for when you are making sushi rice.

WASHING RICE

To improve the flavor and the texture of rice, it's important to wash away any impurities and the *nuka* ("rice bran") before cooking. To wash the rice, put it in a large bowl and cover with cold water. Swish around for a few seconds using your hand, then drain. Do this quickly so the rice doesn't absorb too much of the water with impurities in it. For the second wash, cover with cold water and mix more vigorously, swishing around and rubbing the grains gently with your fingers for about 30 seconds, until the water is cloudy. Drain, cover with cold water, and swish around once more, until the water is less cloudy but not clear. Drain well and use immediately, or cover with cold water and soak for 30 minutes before cooking, a step that adds some subtle textural and nutritional benefits.

Sumeshi, or sushi rice, is Japanese white rice that has been seasoned with sushi zu, a mixture of rice vinegar, salt, and sugar. (In America, Japanese white rice is often referred to as sushi rice, which is inaccurate—it's not "sushi rice" until you season it.) When flavored with sushi zu, the tangy rice enhances whatever goes on top of it—typically raw fish. We use it in our Lox Bowl (page 167) and Temaki Zushi (page 168).

Some chefs argue that rice is the most important part of making sushi. Instead of spending ten years learning how to cook it, you can follow our recipe and become a master in no time! We're kidding, of course, but if you follow these instructions, you can make great sushi rice at home.

MAKES ABOUT 6 CUPS (SERVES 4 TO 6) • TOTAL TIME: 40 MINUTES

In a jar with a tight-fitting lid, stir together the sugar, salt, kombu, and rice vinegar. Cover and let sit at room temperature for a few hours to allow the salt and sugar to dissolve, and let the kombu add its flavor. Sushi zu keeps covered at room temperature for up to 1 year.

If cooking on the stovetop: Put the washed rice into a heavy-duty medium pot with a tight-fitting lid, such as an enameled cast-iron pot like Staub or Le Creuset. Add the 1¾ cups water, cover, and bring to a boil over high heat, 6 to 9 minutes. Do not open the lid—instead, to check if it's boiling, look for steam and listen for bubbling sounds. Immediately reduce the heat to low and cook for exactly 10 minutes. Remove from the heat. Let sit, covered, for 10 minutes.

If using a rice cooker: Put the washed rice in the bowl of a rice cooker. Add enough water to reach the 3 cup line for sushi rice, and cook using the "sushi rice" setting. If your machine does not have the "sushi rice" line and setting, add 1¾ cups water and cook using the white rice setting.

Dump the cooked rice into a large, shallow bowl. While it's steaming-hot, quickly pour on ½ cup plus 1 tablespoon of the sushi zu. Dip a rice paddle in water to prevent the grains from sticking to it, and gently break up the rice with a cutting and folding motion to delicately coax them apart and coat each one in sushi zu, taking care not to break the grains. Simultaneously fan the rice using a Japanese fan or a paper plate so it cools to warm as quickly as possible. The fanning and subsequent cooling of the rice ensures that the steam doesn't get trapped, which would cause the rice to get too soft.

Cover the bowl with a damp towel and set aside until ready to use. The rice is best used while still slightly warm.

Sumeshi

Sushi Rice

酢飯

¾ cup sugar
½ cup plus 1 tablespoon kosher salt
1-inch square of dried kombu
2⅔ cups rice vinegar
2¼ cups (3 rice-cooker cups) Japanese white rice, washed and drained (see Washing Rice, opposite page)
1¾ cups water

Onigiri

おにぎり

6 cups cooked Japanese
　　white rice or multigrain
　　rice (page 215), very warm
Kosher salt
Fillings (recipes follow
　　on page 220): Tuna
　　Mayo Filling, Salted
　　Salmon Filling, or
　　Umeboshi Filling; or
　　¼ to ½ cup Sweet Kombu
　　(page 35)
8 nori sheets, for wrapping
　　(optional)

Variations: Unfilled Onigiri

FURIKAKE ONIGIRI:

Make the rice as directed.
To shape the onigiri, follow
the directions for filled onigiri, but start with ¾ cup of
cooked rice in the bowl and
omit the sprinkling of salt
and the filling. After shaping,
unwrap and sprinkle the
outside of each onigiri all
over with 1 to 1½ teaspoons
of Furikake (page 37). If not
serving immediately, rewrap
in plastic wrap until you are
ready.

YAKI ONIGIRI:

Make the rice as directed.
To shape the onigiri, follow
the directions for filled onigiri, but start with ¾ cup of
cooked rice in the bowl, omit
the filling, and shape the onigiri into triangles. Heat a grill
to medium-high and brush
the grates with vegetable

The word *onigiri* comes from the verb *nigiru,* which means to "hold with your hand." Another name, omusubi, is used widely as well. These rice balls can be stuffed, or have seasonings mixed into the rice before being shaped into either a triangle, a ball, a mini barrel (called a *tawara*), or whatever the shape you like. Onigiri are great with freshly cooked rice, but you can also use leftover rice to make them. If the rice is cold, microwave it for a minute or so until it's warm before you shape it.

This recipe is for basic filled and unfilled onigiri, but feel free to use whatever you think will be good with rice. Some people also wrap the onigiri in nori. When we take them on the go, we bring some sheets and wrap them just as we are about to eat so that the nori stays crispy. The nori adds great flavor and texture, and also keeps your hands from sticking to the rice. Give it a try!

The most traditional way to shape onigiri is by wetting your hands and sprinkling them with salt, then shaping them so the seasoning transfers to the rice. My skin is too sensitive for this, so I shape them using plastic wrap and a bowl. You can also buy onigiri molds, which can make shaping the rice balls even easier. Take care not to pack the rice too tightly: The texture of the onigiri should be *funwari,* or "tender," and not so dense that you can't see the separate grains. **—Sawa**

MAKES 8 ONIGIRI • TOTAL TIME: 15 MINUTES, OR 1 HOUR IF COOKING THE RICE

Make the rice as directed. Prepare a filling(s) of your choice. Prepare a small bowl of water to wet the cup measure and utensils before scooping rice, to prevent it from sticking.

To make the onigiri, start with a small plastic or metal bowl measuring about 1 cup in volume and 4 inches across (don't use ceramic, since the plastic wrap sticks to it). Line with a square piece of plastic wrap, leaving a few inches hanging over the sides. Fill a ½-cup measure with cooked rice. Sprinkle with a little salt, then flip, salted-side down, into the plastic wrap–lined bowl. Using a rice paddle or the back of a spoon, make a small indentation, about the size of the tip of your thumb, in the rice. Place about 1 tablespoon of the filling into the indentation and lightly push it in (❶, page 221). If using umeboshi or sweet kombu, use a little less. Scoop another ¼ cup cooked rice and pat it over the top to seal in the filling (❷, page 221). Sprinkle with a little more salt.

continued

oil. Place the onigiri directly on the grates and grill for a few minutes, until they develop grill marks and start to brown. (The rice should release from the grates once it's browned.) Flip the onigiri and brush with Kombu "Awesome Sauce" (page 35). Grill for a few minutes until grill marks form, then flip again. Brush with the sauce and grill for a few more minutes, until the onigiri starts to caramelize. Flip and grill for another few minutes until the other side caramelizes.

Onigiri, continued

To shape, remove the onigiri from the bowl ❸, and fold the plastic snugly over the rice ❹. To make the triangle shape, use your dominant hand in a cupping shape to form a corner while the other hand shapes the side ❺. Turn the rice ball in your hand two more times to give the onigiri three sides and three corners ❻. Lightly flatten the center of the triangle to finish shaping ❼. For tawara (mini barrel, ❽ and ❾) shape the rice into a cylinder, then gently flatten the top and bottom. A ball shape is pretty intuitive, but take care not to press too hard. Repeat with the remaining rice until you have 8 onigiri. Unwrap when you're ready to eat. Wrap with nori sheets before eating, if you like. Onigiri are best enjoyed at room temperature the day they're made.

Tuna Mayo Filling

4 ounces (about ½ cup) high-quality canned or jarred tuna, drained
1 tablespoon Kewpie mayonnaise
Freshly ground black pepper
Sriracha (optional)

MAKES ENOUGH FOR 8 ONIGIRI

Put the tuna in a small bowl. Using a spoon, break it a bit, then combine thoroughly with the mayonnaise and a few cracks of black pepper. For a spicy tuna filling, stir a few drops of sriracha into the mixture.

Salted Salmon Filling

4 ounces Shiozake (Broiled Salted Salmon, page 54)

MAKES ENOUGH FOR 8 ONIGIRI

Flake the salmon into small pieces to get about ½ cup.

Umeboshi Filling

3 to 5 umeboshi plums

MAKES ENOUGH FOR 8 ONIGIRI

Depending on the size of the plums and how much you want in the onigiri (umeboshi is strong), you might want to use less than other fillings. Remove the pits and gently mash.

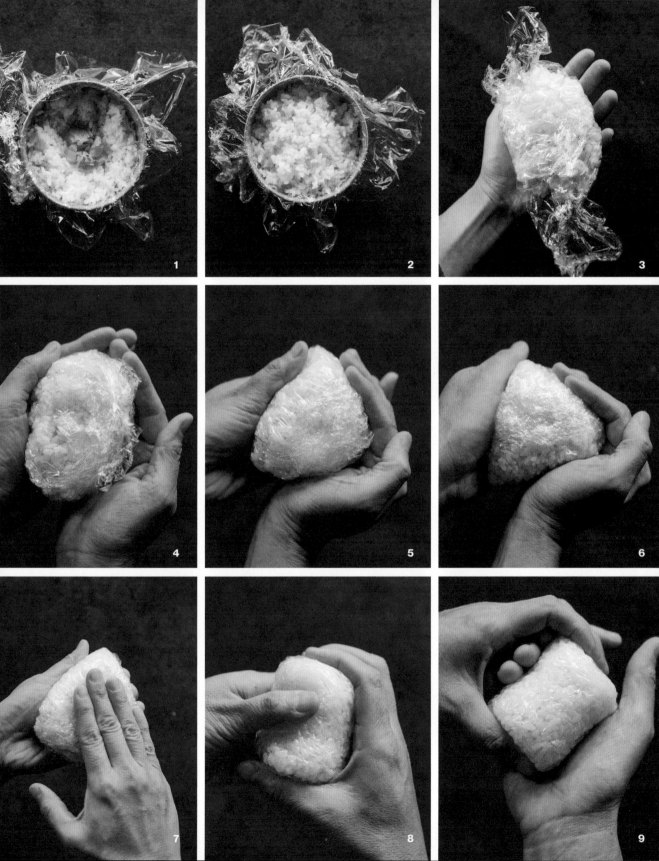

Omurice is leftover rice tossed with vegetables, a bit of meat, and ketchup, topped with a runny omelet and more ketchup. It's a great way to use up leftover rice or other odds and ends in your refrigerator. The ingredients are humble, but when you slice open the omelet and watch it unfold over the rice, revealing a soft, fluffy interior, it can be quite dramatic. The key to the omelet is its loose texture—you want to cook it until it's just set enough to hold its shape when you roll it. If it's too firm or the whole thing falls apart, don't worry, it will still be delicious. For an easier version, you can just cook the omelet into a round crepe shape and flip it out of the pan over the rice, covering it like a blanket, the way my mom used to make it. **—Sawa**

SERVES 4 • TOTAL TIME: 40 MINUTES

To make the rice: In a large frying pan or wok, heat the oil over medium-high heat. Add the chicken and cook, stirring occasionally, until lightly browned, 3 to 5 minutes. Add the onion, carrot, and 1 teaspoon of the salt and cook, stirring often, until the onion is translucent and the carrot has softened just a bit, about 5 minutes. Reduce the heat to low and add the rice, breaking it up with your hands to separate the grains. Stir to break up any remaining lumps. Add the frozen peas and cook for 1 to 2 minutes. Add the ketchup, a few cracks of freshly ground black pepper, and the remaining 1 teaspoon salt and toss to combine.

Remove from the heat and divide evenly among four plates. Shape the rice into ovals about 6 inches long and 4 inches wide.

To make the omelet: In a bowl, whisk together the eggs, milk, and salt. Transfer to a large measuring cup with a pouring spout. In an 8-inch nonstick skillet, heat ½ teaspoon of the butter over high heat, until it starts to sizzle and bubble. Pour in one-quarter of the egg mixture, immediately reduce the heat to its lowest setting, and stir with a silicone spatula to make a very loose scramble. It should be pretty wet. When the bottom of the egg just starts to set, about 30 seconds, start to roll into an omelet shape by tilting the pan at a 30-degree angle and using the spatula to lift and fold the egg onto itself into thirds. Roll the omelet out of the pan, seam-side down, onto one of the ovals of rice so they stack up evenly, one on top of another, like two bricks. (The idea is to make omelets about the size and shape of the rice.) The omelet should be just barely set and still very soft in the middle so when you slice it open, it will drape over the rice. Wipe out the pan and repeat 3 more times with the remaining eggs and butter.

Bring the plates to the table and, using a small, very sharp knife, gently slit the omelets down the center lengthwise, barely grazing the top, so that they open up and drape over the rice. Serve with ketchup, okonomi sauce, or hot sauce.

Omurice

Omelet Rice

オムライス

Rice
2 teaspoons canola oil or vegetable oil
1 boneless, skinless chicken thigh (about 6 ounces), diced small
1 onion, finely diced
1 carrot, peeled and finely diced
2 teaspoons kosher salt
3 cups cooked Japanese White Rice (page 215)
½ cup frozen peas
¼ cup ketchup
Freshly ground black pepper

Omelet
8 eggs
3 tablespoons milk
¾ teaspoon kosher salt
2 teaspoons unsalted butter
Ketchup, okonomi sauce (homemade, page 34, or store-bought, such as Otafuku brand), or your favorite hot sauce, for serving

Mame Gohan

Green Pea Rice

豆ご飯

2 cups water
2-inch square of dried kombu
1 cup green peas, fresh
    or frozen
¼ cup sake
1 teaspoon salt
2¼ cups (3 rice-cooker cups)
    Japanese white rice,
    washed and drained (see
    Washing Rice, page 216)

This simple green pea rice (pictured on page 227) is a great accompaniment to any meal. The key to this recipe is using the cooking liquid from the peas in the rice, lending it a subtle vegetal flavor, and adding the peas at the very end to preserve their bright green color. Mame gohan is especially good in late spring and early summer, when we can get fresh English peas at the farmers' market. They're like little green candies, and taste even sweeter when mixed with white rice. We buy them by the bagful and get our kids to help us shell them, then freeze them so we can always have the taste of springtime on hand.

SERVES 4 TO 6 AS AN ACCOMPANIMENT TO A MEAL • TOTAL TIME: 1 HOUR

In a small pot, combine 2 cups water and kombu and bring to a boil over high heat. If using fresh peas, add to the water and boil for 1 minute. Remove from the heat and let sit for 15 minutes, to allow them to continue cooking and infuse the liquid with pea flavor. If using frozen peas, add to the boiling water, remove from the heat immediately, and let sit for 5 minutes.

If cooking the rice on the stovetop: Reserving the cooking liquid, drain the kombu and peas, and pour the reserved liquid into 4-cup liquid measuring cup. Set the peas aside and discard the kombu (or save it for another use such as Sweet Kombu, page 35). Add the sake and salt to the cooking liquid and top off with water until you have 2½ cups.

Put the washed rice into a heavy-duty medium pot with a tight-fitting lid, such as a Staub or Le Creuset. Add the cooking liquid mixture, cover, and bring to a boil over high heat, 6 to 9 minutes. Do not open the lid—instead, to check if it's boiling, look for steam and listen for bubbling sounds. Immediately reduce the heat to low and cook for exactly 10 minutes. Remove from the heat. Let sit, covered, for 10 minutes.

If cooking the rice in a rice cooker: Put the washed rice in the bowl of a rice cooker. Drain the cooking liquid from the peas and kombu directly into the rice cooker bowl. Set the peas aside and discard the cooked kombu (or reserve for another use, such as Sweet Kombu, page 35). Add the sake, salt, and enough water to reach the 3-cup line for white rice. Cook on the white rice setting.

When the rice is finished cooking, open the lid and add the reserved peas. Dip a rice paddle in water to prevent the grains from sticking to it, then fluff the rice and mix in the peas by scooping down to the bottom and gently folding up a few times. Some steam will be released and the rice will be more aerated.

Scoop into four or six bowls, depending on how many people you are serving.

This mushroom rice (pictured on page 227) is great for when you want a little more than rice with your meal. We like to use a mix of earthy maitake (hen of the woods), meaty shiitake, and silky shimeji (beech), our son's favorite. Find a blend you love. Cremini, button mushrooms, oyster mushrooms, chanterelles, morels, black trumpets, all of them will work. For a more luxurious version, you can use matsutake, the most prized of Japanese mushrooms. They are meaty, floral, and very expensive, so use half the amount—a little goes a long way. Leftovers are wonderful in a bento or shaped into Onigiri (page 218).

SERVES 4 TO 6 AS AN ACCOMPANIMENT TO A MEAL • TOTAL TIME: 40 MINUTES

If cooking the rice on the stovetop: Put the washed rice into a heavy-duty medium pot with a tight-fitting lid, such as a Staub or Le Creuset braiser. Add the 2¼ cups plus 1 tablespoon water, sake, mirin, soy sauce, salt, and kombu. Stir to combine. Gently lay the mushrooms over the rice. Cover and bring to a boil over high heat, 6 to 9 minutes. Do not open the lid—instead, to check if it's boiling, look for steam and listen for bubbling sounds. Immediately reduce the heat to low and cook for exactly 10 minutes. Remove from the heat. Let sit, covered, for 10 minutes.

If cooking the rice in a rice cooker: Put the washed rice in the bowl of a rice cooker. Add the sake, mirin, and soy sauce. Pour enough water to reach the 3-cup line for white rice. Stir in the salt and kombu. Gently lay the mushrooms over the rice and cook on the white rice setting.

When the rice is finished cooking, carefully open the lid. Dip a rice paddle in water to prevent the grains from sticking to it. Fluff the rice by scooping down to the bottom and gently folding up a few times. Some steam will be released and the rice will be more aerated. Remove the kombu.

Scoop into four or six bowls, depending on how many people you are serving.

Mushroom Rice

きのこご飯

2¼ cups (3 rice-cooker cups) Japanese white rice, washed and drained (see Washing Rice, page 216)

2¼ cups plus 1 tablespoon water (if cooking on the stovetop)

1 tablespoon sake

1 tablespoon mirin

1 tablespoon soy sauce

1 teaspoon kosher salt

2-inch square of dried kombu or ½ teaspoon dashi powder

4 cups mixed mushrooms (such as maitake, shiitake caps, shimeji, cremini, or button), cleaned and cut or torn into small bite-size pieces

Hijiki and Carrot Rice

ひじきご飯

2 tablespoons dried hijiki
2¼ cups (3 rice-cooker cups)
   Japanese white rice,
   washed and drained (see
   Washing Rice, page 216)
2½ cups Dashi (page 33)
   or 2½ teaspoons dashi
   powder mixed into
   2½ cups water
1 tablespoon kosher salt
1 cup grated carrot

When our son was very young and resistant to eating vegetables, we'd sneak him some by adding hijiki and grated carrots to his rice. It's a great way to smuggle nutrition to a carb-loving two-year-old. Fortunately, he outgrew that phase by age three, but this dish has remained a family favorite. It's an easy way to make dinner a little more exciting. The carrots add some sweetness, while the hijiki has a mild ocean flavor, and they look so pretty in white rice. This goes well with just about any fish or vegetable dish. We recommend making Onigiri (page 218) with the leftovers.

SERVES 4 TO 6 AS AN ACCOMPANIMENT TO A MEAL • TOTAL TIME: 40 MINUTES

In a small bowl, soak the dried hijiki in about 1 cup of room-temperature water for 10 minutes, until it has expanded to about eight times its original size. Drain, rinse, and drain again. Set aside.

If cooking the rice on the stovetop: Put the washed rice into a heavy-duty medium pot with a tight-fitting lid, such as Staub or Le Creuset. Add the dashi and salt and stir to combine. Place the grated carrot and drained hijiki over the rice in an even layer. Cover and bring to a boil over high heat, 6 to 9 minutes. Do not open the lid—instead, to check if it's boiling, look for steam and listen for bubbling sounds. Immediately reduce the heat to low and cook for exactly 10 minutes. Remove from the heat. Let sit, covered, for 10 minutes.

If cooking the rice in a rice cooker: Put the washed rice in the bowl of a rice cooker. Add the dashi. It should reach the 3-cup line for white rice. Stir in the salt. Distribute the grated carrot and hijiki evenly over the rice. Cook on the white rice setting.

When the rice is finished cooking, carefully open the lid. Dip a rice paddle in water to prevent the grains from sticking to it. Fluff the rice and mix in the hijiki and carrots by scooping down to the bottom and gently folding up a few times. Some steam will be released and the rice will become more aerated.

Scoop into four or six bowls, depending on how many people you are serving.

We love eating this easy salmon rice for breakfast, lunch, or dinner. Pair it with miso soup and you have a wonderful meal. It's a great way to use up leftover Bonito-Cured Lox (page 163) or extra Shiozake (page 54), and it works well with fresh salmon, too. Some people remove the skin, but we enjoy how soft it gets once it's cooked, and mix it right into the rice. To top it off, we add heaps of ikura, which is salmon roe. The more you put on, the more decadent the dish will be. Ikura also happens to be our kids' favorite food. They just love how the salty little eggs pop in their mouths.

SERVES 4 • TOTAL TIME: 40 MINUTES

If cooking the rice on the stovetop: Put the washed rice into a heavy-duty medium pot with a tight-fitting lid, such as Staub or Le Creuset. Add the 2½ cups water. Sprinkle in the dashi powder (or add the kombu). Lay the salmon, skin-side up, on top of the rice and cover with the lid. Bring to a boil over high heat, 6 to 9 minutes. Do not open the lid—instead, to check if it's boiling, look for steam and listen for bubbling sounds. Immediately reduce the heat to low and cook for exactly 10 minutes. Remove from the heat. Let sit, covered, for 10 minutes.

If cooking the rice in a rice cooker: Place the washed rice in the bowl of a rice cooker. Add enough water to reach the 3-cup line for white rice. Sprinkle in the dashi powder or lay in the kombu. Lay the salmon, skin-side up, on the rice, and cook on the white rice setting.

When the rice is finished cooking, carefully open the lid. Dip a rice paddle in water to prevent the grains from sticking to it. Fluff the rice and flake apart the salmon by scooping down to the bottom and gently folding up a few times. Some steam will be released and the rice will become more aerated. Remove the kombu, if that's what you used.

Scoop the rice into four or six bowls, depending on how many people you are serving. Top with the ikura, drizzle with soy sauce, and sprinkle with the scallions and torn nori.

Salmon and Ikura Rice

イクラ鮭ご飯

2¼ cups (3 rice-cooker cups) Japanese white rice, washed and drained (see Washing Rice, page 216)

2½ cups water (if cooking on the stovetop)

1 teaspoon dashi powder or 2-inch square of kombu

6 ounces salted salmon (Bonito-Cured Lox, page 163, or Shiozake, page 54), or fresh salmon seasoned with 1 teaspoon salt

¼ cup ikura (salmon roe)

Soy sauce, for drizzling

2 scallions, thinly sliced

1 sheet nori (optional), torn into small pieces or shredded

Tori Gobo Gohan

Chicken and Burdock Rice

鳥ごぼうご飯

1 pound boneless, skin-on (if possible) chicken thighs, cut into ¾-inch cubes

2 tablespoons shio koji

6-inch piece of gobo (burdock root), cut from the thick side

2¼ cups (3 rice-cooker cups) Japanese white rice, washed and drained (see Washing Rice, page 216)

2⅓ cups chicken stock (or dashi, homemade, page 33, or 2½ teaspoons dashi powder mixed into 2⅓ cups water)

1-inch piece of fresh ginger, sliced into thirds

2 tablespoons sake

1½ tablespoons soy sauce, plus more for serving

2 scallions, thinly sliced

1 sheet nori, torn or shredded

Rice, chicken, and gobo (burdock root) are often eaten together in Japan, with good reason. Toothsome gobo complements the rice, which absorbs the juices from the chicken. We marinate it in shio koji, which adds an element of umami and tenderizes the meat. Then there's the okoge, which we love—a browned, crunchy, caramelized bottom layer of rice that you can only achieve if you cook it on the stovetop.

SERVES 4 • TOTAL TIME: 40 MINUTES

In a small bowl, mix the chicken with the shio koji. Cover and refrigerate. This can be done as few as 15 minutes before cooking or up to 1 day in advance.

Fill a bowl with cold water. Use the back of a knife to scrape off the brown outer layer of the gobo. Using a vegetable peeler or a sharp paring knife, slice 1- to 2-inch long shavings of gobo directly into the water so it doesn't oxidize (the flesh turns brown almost immediately after you cut it). Think of this like sharpening a pencil, going around and rotating each time after you make a shaving. When it gets too small to use a peeler, use a knife to thinly slice.

If cooking the rice on the stovetop: Put the washed rice into a heavy-duty medium pot with a tight-fitting lid, such as Staub or Le Creuset. Add the chicken stock, ginger, sake, and soy sauce and stir to combine. Drain the gobo very well and squeeze out as much moisture as you can. Place over the rice in an even layer (do not mix it in), then place the chicken gently over the gobo. Cover and bring to a boil over high heat, 6 to 9 minutes. Do not open the lid—instead, to check if it's boiling, look for steam and listen for bubbling sounds. Immediately reduce the heat to low and cook for exactly 10 minutes. To get okoge (the crispy browned bottom layer), increase the heat to medium-high and cook for 3 minutes. Remove from the heat. Let sit, covered, for 10 minutes.

If cooking the rice in a rice cooker: Put the washed rice in the bowl of a rice cooker. Add the chicken stock, ginger, sake, and soy sauce and stir to combine. Drain the gobo very well and squeeze out as much moisture as you can. Place over the rice in an even layer (do not mix it in), then place the chicken gently over the gobo. Cook on the white rice setting.

When the rice is finished cooking, carefully open the lid. Dip a rice paddle in water to help prevent the grains from sticking to it. Fluff the rice and mix in the gobo and chicken by scooping down to the bottom and gently folding up a few times (if making the stovetop version, you will also be folding in bits of okoge). Some steam will be released and the rice will be more aerated. Pick out the ginger and discard.

Scoop the rice into four bowls. Sprinkle the scallions and nori on top. Season with a little soy sauce and serve.

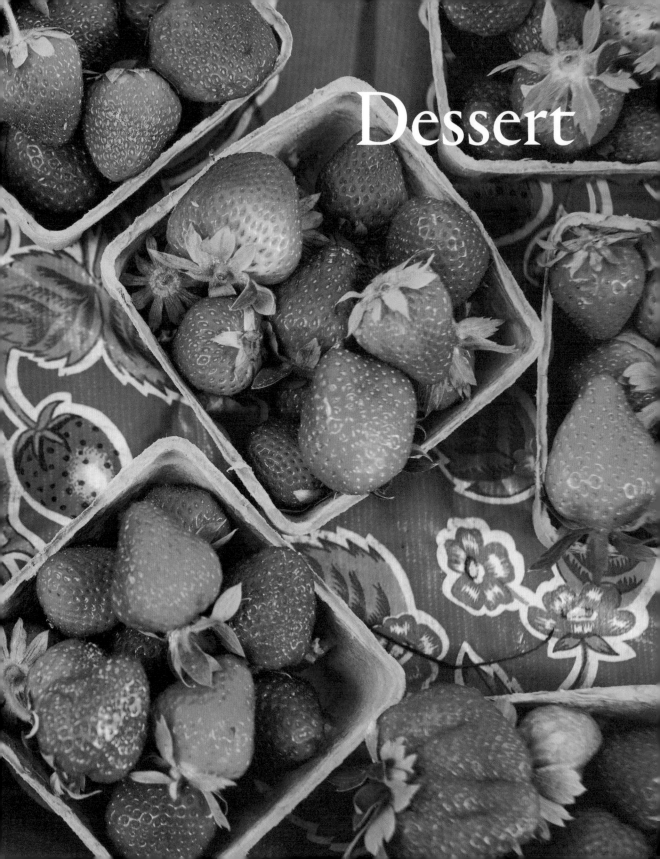

Dessert

デザート

Though desserts in Japan are sweet, many incorporate savory ingredients that introduce balance and complexity. Take matcha, with its bitter and grassy flavor. Or starchy adzuki beans, which are cooked and sweetened with sugar. Sesame also makes its way into traditional desserts, as do sweet potatoes. Sometimes, dessert might simply consist of fruit at its peak. There has also been a big demand in recent decades for Western-style pastries. French-influenced strawberry shortcake—a fluffy layer cake with whipped cream and ripe strawberries—is the country's most beloved dessert, and what we make for our daughter on her birthday.

We like to have some dough for these super-simple matcha cookies in the freezer at all times. They're like soft, tender sugar cookies with green tea flavor. Just thaw, slice, and bake. Matcha, a powder made from ground green tea leaves, adds a bit of bitterness to offset the sweetness. These cookies were originally used for ice cream sandwiches at our restaurant. Feel free to stack them with your favorite scoop, or snack on them with coffee, tea, or milk. If you want to get creative, mix-ins like white chocolate chips or macadamia nuts go great with matcha.

Matcha does have a shelf life. Check the sell-by date when you purchase it to make sure it's fresh. After you open the package, store it in an airtight container in the freezer to maintain its beautiful aroma and vibrant color, and try to use it within a few months.

MAKES ABOUT 40 COOKIES • ACTIVE TIME: 30 MINUTES • TOTAL TIME: 2 HOURS 40 MINUTES, INCLUDING CHILLING THE COOKIE DOUGH

In a stand mixer fitted with the whisk, beat the butter on medium-high speed until creamy, 2 to 3 minutes. Turn the mixer off, add the brown sugar and granulated sugar, then increase the speed to medium-high and whisk until thoroughly combined and fluffy, 3 to 4 minutes. Scrape down the sides of the bowl, then add the honey, egg, and vanilla. Whisk on medium-high until the ingredients are fully incorporated. Remove the mixing bowl from the machine.

Sift the flour, baking soda, salt, and matcha powder over a large bowl or a large piece of parchment paper. Add the dry ingredients to the wet ingredients all at once, then fold them in using a large spatula, until the flour is just blended. Do not overmix.

Prepare four pieces of plastic wrap, each measuring about 12 × 12 inches. Divide the dough into 4 equal portions and place one in the center of each square of plastic wrap. Shape the dough into a rough log about 8 inches long. Fold the plastic over the log the long way, then shape into a uniform cylinder, gently smoothing and rolling, until the log is about 10 inches long and a uniform width. Twist the ends of the plastic tightly. This should compress the log back to about 8 inches. Repeat with the remaining 3 portions of dough. Refrigerate for at least 2 hours until completely chilled, or freeze in a resealable freezer bag for up to 3 months, and place in the refrigerator 1 hour before baking.

Preheat the oven to 350°F. Line a baking sheet with parchment paper.

continued

Slice-and-Bake Matcha Cookies

抹茶クッキー

170g (12 tablespoons) unsalted butter, at room temperature

100g (½ cup) packed light brown sugar

100g (½ cup) granulated sugar

80g (¼ cup) honey

1 large egg, at room temperature

½ teaspoon vanilla extract

335g (2¼ cups) all-purpose flour

½ teaspoon baking soda

¼ teaspoon salt

15g (1 tablespoon) high-quality matcha powder

Remove a log from the refrigerator. Slice into 10 equal pieces, roughly ½ to ¾ inch thick. Place on the baking sheet about 2 inches apart, then press down on each cookie using the palm of your hand, shaping it into a 2-inch disk. The cookies should have at least 1 inch separating them. If you are baking more than one log, repeat this step as needed.

Bake until the cookies are puffy but not browned, 5 to 6 minutes. (If you are baking two sheets at a time, switch their positions and rotate halfway through.) Let cool on the baking sheet to set, about 10 minutes. Transfer to a cooling rack and cool completely. The cookies should be soft and slightly chewy. They will keep in an airtight container at room temperature for a week.

Chocolate-Banana Milk Bread Pudding

We love this bread pudding recipe because it combines two things that go well together: dark chocolate and banana. It's also a smart way to use up stale bread and old bananas (like, really dark skin and mushy flesh). Here we use Shokupan (page 97), but other soft sandwich breads such as challah, brioche, or white bread will all work. It's delicious warm, right after it's baked. If you have leftovers, slice and reheat in a skillet with a little bit of butter. It tastes almost like French toast.

チョコバナナブレッドプディング

Put the bread in a bowl. Pour in the melted butter and sprinkle with 2 teaspoons of the sugar. Toss together using your hands and set aside.

In a bowl, whisk the eggs and the remaining 6 tablespoons sugar together until fully incorporated and the mixture turns pale yellow, 1 to 2 minutes.

In a small pot, combine the cream, milk, cinnamon, and salt. Warm over medium heat until small bubbles form at the edges of the pot, turning off the heat just before it is about to boil. Whisking constantly so you don't scramble the eggs, slowly pour the cream mixture into the egg mixture, starting with a drizzle and gradually increasing to a thin, steady stream. Stir in the vanilla, then strain the mixture through a fine-mesh sieve into the bowl with the bread. Toss a few times so the bread is well coated. Cover and refrigerate for at least 3 hours, or up to 2 days before baking. This will ensure that the bread has fully soaked up the custard.

Preheat the oven to 325°F. Coat a 9 × 5-inch loaf pan with cooking spray or grease with oil. Cut a piece of parchment paper to fit the bottom of the pan and smooth it onto the pan.

Fold the chocolate and banana into the bread mixture until well distributed. Transfer to the prepared pan and spread in an even layer. Give it a few taps on a hard surface to get any air pockets out. Bake for 45 minutes to 1 hour, rotating the pan front to back halfway through. Start checking for doneness at 45 minutes by sticking a cake tester or the tip of a knife into the center. If it comes out clean and the top and edges are a light golden brown, it's done (a little melted chocolate is okay, but you shouldn't see any custard). If not, bake in 5-minute increments, up to 15 minutes longer, until a cake tester comes out clean. Remove from the oven and let cool for at least 30 minutes in the pan.

To serve, run a butter knife around the edges to release the sides. Flip over onto a cutting board and slice while still warm. Serve immediately as is, or with a dollop of whipped cream or crème fraîche. The bread pudding will keep, refrigerated, for up to 1 week.

5 cups stale Shokupan (page 97) or other soft sandwich bread, crusts removed and cut into ½-inch cubes

2 tablespoons unsalted butter, melted

6 tablespoons plus 2 teaspoons sugar

2 large eggs

1 cup heavy cream

⅓ cup whole milk

⅛ teaspoon ground cinnamon

Pinch of kosher salt

½ teaspoon vanilla extract

Cooking spray or neutral oil, such as canola oil or vegetable oil, for the pan

¼ cup bittersweet chocolate chips (preferably 72% cacao)

1 overripe banana, cut into slices ¼ inch thick

Whipped cream or crème fraîche (optional), for serving

Strawberry Shortcake

苺ショートケーキ

Sponge Cake
Cooking spray or butter
   and flour, for the pan
148g (1 cup) cake flour
42g (⅓ cup) cornstarch
6 large eggs, at room
   temperature
150g (¾ cup) sugar
70g (5 tablespoons) unsalted
   butter, melted and
   very warm

Soaking Syrup
1 cup (236g) water
38g (3 tablespoons) sugar
2 teaspoons kirsch or
   a liqueur such as
   Grand Marnier

Topping
2 cups heavy cream,
   very cold
50g (¼ cup) sugar
1 (16-ounce) container
   strawberries, hulled
   and halved, reserving
   6 to 8 for decorating

Strawberry shortcake (or ichigo short in Japanese) is the cake of cakes in Japan. No other comes even close. The combination of airy sponge cake, sweet and light chantilly (whipped cream), and tart and juicy strawberries that match the color of the Japanese flag have captured people's hearts. It's been the most popular cake for birthdays and Christmas celebrations for as long as I can remember. This classic recipe was adapted from a recipe by my friend, the pastry chef Ayako Watanabe. —**Sawa**

SERVES 6 TO 8 • ACTIVE TIME: 1 HOUR • TOTAL TIME: 3 HOURS TO OVERNIGHT, INCLUDING CHILLING

To make the sponge cake: Preheat the oven to 325°F. Mist a 9-inch round cake pan with cooking spray, line the sides with a strip of parchment paper that matches the height of the pan, and line the bottom of the pan with a 9-inch parchment round; or butter and flour the pan.

In a bowl, stir together the cake flour and cornstarch. Sift twice into a second bowl or onto a sheet of parchment and set aside.

In a stand mixer fitted with the whisk, beat the eggs and sugar on high speed until pale and foamy, about 2 minutes. Reduce the speed to medium and beat for about 3 minutes, then reduce to low and mix until the batter leaves a ribbon-like trace when you lift the whisk, about 1 minute longer.

Sift the flour mixture again, this time directly into the batter. Using a large rubber spatula, fold in the dry ingredients by hand until just combined, taking care not to deflate the batter. In a small bowl, add about ½ cup of the batter to the melted butter and stir to combine. Add the butter mixture to the rest of the batter, folding gently until just combined.

Pour the batter into the prepared pan, filling it two-thirds of the way. You may have more batter than can fit in the pan, but that's okay, you can discard it or bake a tiny cake for snacking. Rap the pan on the countertop to knock out large air bubbles.

Bake until the cake is golden and a tester inserted in the center comes out clean, 30 to 40 minutes. Rap the pan on the countertop once more, then invert onto a cooling rack and let cool, upside-down, in the pan. (Cooling the cake inverted in the pan makes it less likely to collapse and keeps it moister.)

continued

To make the soaking syrup: In a small pot, combine the 1 cup water and sugar and bring to a boil, stirring to dissolve. Remove from the heat, stir in the kirsch and let cool.

Unmold the cooled sponge, remove the parchment, invert the cake onto a clean surface, and split horizontally into 2 equal layers.

To make the topping: In a stand mixer fitted with the whisk (or in a large bowl with a whisk if mixing by hand), whip the cream and sugar together on low speed for about 3 minutes. When the cream starts to thicken, increase to medium and whip until almost stiff, about 30 seconds longer.

Place the bottom layer of the cake on a cake decorating turntable or a serving plate. Using a pastry brush, moisten the first layer generously with syrup. Using an offset spatula, spread on one-quarter of the whipped cream in an even layer. Cover with the strawberry halves, cut-side up, leaving no gaps. Spread another one-quarter of the cream over the strawberries. Cover with the second layer of sponge and moisten it generously with more syrup. Frost the top and sides of the cake with the remaining whipped cream. Decorate with the reserved strawberries. Refrigerate for at least 2 hours or up to overnight before serving.

In the fall, we go apple picking at a local orchard and come home with more apples than we know what to do with. Without fail, I make this buttery upside-down cake with my favorite Fuji apples. They're sturdy enough to bake, with a good balance of tartness and sweetness. I love the reveal when you flip the cake over and see the once-hidden golden brown apples adorning the top. When making the caramel for the topping, resist the urge to stir, which can cause the sugar to crystallize. Just shake the pot a bit to help coax the melting along. If the caramel turns crumbly, don't fret—you can still use it. **—Sawa**

SERVES 6 TO 8 • ACTIVE TIME: 30 MINUTES • TOTAL TIME: 1½ HOURS

Preheat the oven to 350°F. Mist the sides of a 9-inch round cake pan with cooking spray.

To make the caramel: In a small pot, combine the brown sugar, butter, and honey and heat over medium heat. Do not stir. Gently shake the pan to help melt the butter and the sugar. Once the mixture turns to liquid, cook until it starts to bubble and develop a nice amber color, 3 to 4 minutes, then immediately remove from the heat. Carefully pour into the prepared cake pan (it's very hot!) and set aside.

To make the cake: Put the apples cut-side down on a cutting board and slice straight down into ¼-inch-thick half-moons. Starting at the outer edge of the pan and working your way toward the center, layer the apple slices on top of the caramel in a pinwheel shape, with each slice overlapping just a bit. Cut any leftover slices into small cubes to add to the batter later. Finely zest the yuzu over the apples. Squeeze 1 tablespoon of juice from the yuzu, sprinkle over the apples, and set the pan aside.

In a small bowl, mix the flour, baking powder, and salt until well combined. Set aside.

In a stand mixer fitted with the whisk, beat the eggs on high speed until very frothy, 3 to 4 minutes. Add the granulated sugar and continue mixing on high speed until the mixture looks shiny, another 5 minutes. Add the rum, vanilla, and cinnamon and mix on low speed for a few seconds, just to incorporate. Remove the bowl from the machine.

Fuji Apple Upside-Down Cake

ふじりんご
アップサイドダウンケーキ

Cooking spray or a neutral oil, for the pan

Caramel
100g (½ cup) packed light brown sugar
57g (4 tablespoons) unsalted butter
1 tablespoon honey

Cake
2 Fuji apples, peeled, cored, and halved through the core
1 fresh yuzu, Meyer lemon, or lemon
250g (1¾ cups) all-purpose flour, sifted
1½ teaspoons baking powder
Pinch of kosher salt
4 large eggs, at room temperature
250g (1¼ cups) granulated sugar
1 tablespoon dark rum
½ teaspoon vanilla extract
¼ teaspoon ground cinnamon
225g (16 tablespoons/2 sticks) unsalted butter, melted and cooled to room temperature

Vanilla ice cream (optional), for serving

continued

Using a rubber spatula, fold in one-third of the flour mixture until just incorporated. Add half of the melted butter and fold to incorporate. Fold in another one-third of the flour mixture until just incorporated. Add the remaining melted butter, folding just a few times. Fold in the remaining flour mixture and the cubed apples until just incorporated. Fold a few more times, then pour the batter into the pan and spread in an even layer.

Bake until a cake tester inserted in the center comes out clean, 50 minutes to 1 hour. Transfer to a cooling rack to cool in the pan until it is no longer hot, but still warm, 30 minutes to 1 hour. Slide a butter knife around where the cake meets the pan to help loosen the edges. Flip the cake over onto a platter and give it a tap to unmold. Slice and serve immediately with vanilla ice cream, if desired. Stored in an airtight container, the cake can keep for up to 1 week in the refrigerator.

I love the textures of this simple parfait—melty matcha ice cream, chewy mochi balls, jelly-like canned peaches, chunky adzuki (red bean) paste, and crunchy graham cracker crumbs (for a fancier black sesame crumb layer, see page 248). It looks so good in a tall glass. For the mochi balls, you need shiratamako flour, a coarse glutinous rice flour that forms a dough that stays soft even when it's cold. This kind of mochi is easy to make: just a mix of shiratamako and water rolled into balls and blanched in boiling water. They puff up after cooking and are soft but bouncy, kind of like those tapioca balls from Asian tea parlors, but with the flavor of sweet rice.

You can buy shiratamako flour, adzuki paste, and kokuto sugar (Japanese black sugar, which usually comes in rock form) at most Asian or Japanese markets. If you can't find kokuto, Grandma's brand molasses is similar to the syrup I make for the parfait. Just pour a bit on top and enjoy. **—Sawa**

SERVES 4 • TOTAL TIME: 20 MINUTES

To make the mochi balls: Place the shiratamako in a small bowl, add the ¼ cup water, and mix well by hand. When the dough comes together after a minute or two, it should feel similar to an earlobe and no longer stick to your hands. Divide into 16 equal portions and roll into marble-size balls using your palms. It should feel like Play-Doh. If the dough is too wet or dry, adjust by adding a drop or two of water if dry, or a pinch or two of shiratamako if too wet.

Bring a pot of water to a boil over high heat. Prepare an ice bath by filling a small bowl with cold water and ice cubes.

Drop the mochi balls one by one into the boiling water. Let the water come back to boil and cook for 2 to 3 minutes. When the mochi balls float up to the surface, stir a few times to let them swim, then cook for 2 to 3 minutes longer. Use a slotted spoon or a small strainer to scoop up the mochi balls and drop them into the ice bath. Let them cool and keep in the water until ready to assemble. A fully cooked mochi ball should be chewy, with no dry dough left in the center.

To make the kokuto syrup: In a small pot, bring the ¼ cup plus 1 tablespoon water to a boil. Add the kokuto sugar, remove from the heat, and stir well to melt and incorporate. Set the syrup aside.

To assemble the parfaits: Drop 1 tablespoon of graham cracker crumbs into the bottom of each of four parfait glasses. Place a scoop of matcha ice cream on top. Spoon a few teaspoons of adzuki paste over the ice cream. Drop in 2 mochi balls and 2 peach slices. Add one more layer of graham cracker crumbs, ice cream, adzuki paste, mochi balls, and peach slices. Drizzle 1 tablespoon of the kokuto syrup on top. Serve immediately.

Matcha Parfait

抹茶パフェ

Mochi Balls
⅓ cup plus 2 tablespoons (60g) shiratamako (glutinous rice flour), such as Tamasan brand
¼ cup (60g) water

Kokuto Syrup
¼ cup plus 1 tablespoon (70g) water
10 nickel-size pieces (50g) kokuto sugar

Parfait
½ cup crumbled graham crackers or your favorite cookies, crushed into pea-size bits
1 pint matcha or green tea ice cream, such as Häagen-Dazs or Maeda-en brand
1 (7-ounce) can tsubuan (chunky sweet adzuki bean paste), such as Imuraya brand
4 canned no-sugar-added peach halves, such as Dole, sliced into quarters

Satsumaimo Cheesecake

さつまいもチーズケーキ

560g (20 ounces) Japanese
　　sweet potatoes (about 2),
　　washed
Softened butter, for the pan

Sesame Crust
140g graham crackers
　　(nine 5 × 2½-inch graham
　　crackers; 1 sleeve from
　　a 14.4-ounce box)
80g (6 tablespoons) unsalted
　　butter, melted
20g (1 tablespoon plus
　　2 teaspoons) kuro neri
　　goma (black sesame paste)
　　or tahini
2 teaspoons sugar
¼ teaspoon kosher salt

Batter
180g (¾ cup) whole-milk
　　ricotta
40g (1½ ounces) cream
　　cheese, at room
　　temperature
100g (½ cup) sugar
100g (½ cup) sour cream
2 teaspoons cornstarch
2 large eggs
⅔ cup heavy cream
⅛ teaspoon ground cinnamon
Finely grated zest of ½ lemon
¼ teaspoon vanilla extract
Boiling water

Lightly sweetened whipped
　　cream or crème fraîche,
　　for serving

It's common to use satsumaimo (Japanese sweet potatoes) in desserts in Japan. There's one that in Japanese is simply called *sweet potato*, a baked mixture of mashed sweet potatoes, sugar, butter, and cream. That's what this cheesecake reminds me of. Sweet potatoes add body and earthy flavor to the filling, and complement the nutty sesame crust. It's less rich and sweet than your classic cheesecake, but still luxurious. If you can't find satsumaimo (Japanese sweet potatoes), just use the American kind. The batter will be slightly wetter, so add an extra teaspoon of cornstarch to achieve the right consistency.

I also love using the black sesame crust mixture as a crumble in place of graham crackers in the Matcha Parfait (page 247). Just spread over a sheet pan and bake at 350°F until dry and sandy, 7 to 10 minutes.

SERVES 6 TO 8 • ACTIVE TIME: 30 MINUTES • TOTAL TIME: 3 HOURS

Preheat the oven to 375°F.

Wrap each sweet potato tightly in foil and bake until fork-tender, 1½ to 2 hours, turning halfway through. Cool for about 15 minutes. Unwrap and peel the sweet potatoes, then mash in a small bowl. Measure out 400g (1½ cups) and set aside. Save the rest for another use. Leave the oven on.

Generously butter a 9-inch springform pan. Line the bottom with a round of parchment paper, smoothing it so it sticks. Wrap the outside of the pan with foil to prevent water from seeping in while it bakes in the water bath. Set aside.

To make the sesame crust: In a food processor, pulse the graham crackers a few times until the consistency of cornmeal. In a small bowl, mix the melted butter and kuro neri goma. Pour into the food processor, pulsing a few times to incorporate. Add the sugar and salt and pulse a few times to combine.

Transfer the graham cracker mixture to the prepared springform pan. Using your fingers, push the crumbs firmly into the bottom of the pan, creating an even thickness. The crust can be made and refrigerated up to 1 week ahead, or frozen for up to 2 months.

To make the batter: In a food processor, process the ricotta and cream cheese until smooth, about 1 minute. Add the sugar, pulse for 30 seconds, scrape down the sides with a spatula, and process for another minute. Add the sour cream and cornstarch, pulse for 30 seconds, then process for 1 minute. Add the eggs and process until incorporated, about 1 minute. Add the mashed sweet

continued

potato and process until fully blended, 1 to 2 minutes, scraping down the sides of the bowl once or twice. Add the heavy cream, cinnamon, lemon zest, and vanilla and blend until incorporated.

Pour the batter through a fine-mesh sieve over a large bowl (it should look like a thin pancake batter), pushing it through with a spatula. Pour into the crust, smooth out the top with a spatula, and gently rap on the counter to get out any air bubbles. Place in a large roasting pan and set on a pulled-out rack in the oven. Pour boiling water into the roasting pan to come halfway up the sides of the springform pan.

Bake for 25 minutes. Rotate the pan front to back and bake until a skewer inserted in the center comes out clean, 25 to 30 minutes longer. Remove from the oven, taking care not to splash the water. Transfer the cheesecake to a cooling rack, remove the foil, and let cool to room temperature. Cover and refrigerate overnight to set.

When ready to serve, unmold the cake, slice, and serve with whipped cream.

Sources

These are some of our favorite sources for Japanese ingredients and equipment; many of them ship nationally.

H Mart (hmart.com): Asian groceries

Japan Premium Beef (japanpremiumbeef.com): Supplier of wagyu beef

Japan Village (japanvillage.com, pictured): Japanese groceries and kitchenware

Kayanoya USA (usa.kayanoya.com): Quality dashi powder

Korin (korin.com): Japanese kitchenware and knives

Masamoto (masamoto-sohonten. co.jp): Award-winning Japanese knives

Mitsuwa (mitsuwa.com): Japanese groceries

MTC Kitchen (mtckitchen.com): Japanese dry goods, kitchenware, and knives

Nagomi (eshop.mitsuboshi-cutlery. com): Japanese knives, including excellent bread knives

The Rice Factory (trf-ny.com): Japanese rice and specialty dry goods

Sunrise Mart (sunrisemart.com): Japanese groceries

Suzuki Farm (suzukifarm-usa.com): Mail-order Japanese produce

Toiro Kitchen (toirokitchen.com): Japanese kitchen tools and hotpots

Acknowledgments

Before we break off into our individual thank-yous, we want to extend our bottomless gratitude to the testers who helped us make our recipes better than we ever could have on our own: Liz Alpern, Danielle Brodsky, Amorette Casaus, Carter Edwards, Lisa Freedman, Anna Gershenson, Darra Goldstein, Kaori Goto, Andi Grossman, Emily Iguchi, Heather Israel, Shira Kline, Leah Koenig, Min Kong, Abbie Kozolochyk, Bernard Kravitz, Nicole Marino, Rebecca Flint Marx, Lisa Masuda, Cecily McAndrews, Lupin Mindlin, Thierry Morpurgo, Alex Roberts, Eri Shoji, Adina Steiman, Eric Takahashi, Melissa Uchiyama, Inga Veksler, Adan Velis, Alexa Weibel, and Jeffrey Yoskowitz.

From Sawa and Aaron: We love doing our "thankful of the day" at the dinner table with our family, something we started during the pandemic stay-home period. We just thank whatever happened that day, taking turns, and repeating each other mostly with slight variations since we did the same thing together. We are so grateful for being given the opportunity to write this book.

We spent countless hours meeting with Gabi. Writing is both joyous and stomach churning at times. We have a lot of respect for Gabi for doing so as her profession. Thank you for wanting to help us tell our story. Without your talent, expertise, passion, incredible eye for detail, and ability to get the best out of us, this book wouldn't have happened.

Thank you to our agent, Sarah Smith, for your perseverance, and the David Black Agency for thinking our story was worth telling and connecting us with such amazing talent. To all the wonderful people at Ten Speed Press, our amazing editor, Kelly Snowden, who took an interest in our project and has guided us through this process with such expertise and warmth. To the incredibly talented designer, Lizzie Allen, for making this book come to life, and Yuki Sugiura for your beautiful photographs and equal love of oden. Thank you, Suzie Myers, for your wonderful passion for plateware and vegetable still lifes, and Lisa Masuda—and your magical heat gun that helped make the food in this book look incredible. And thank you to other amazing cookbook authors, Darra Goldstein, Leah Koenig, and Jeffrey Yoskowitz, who gave us their time and shared their expertise.

To all the people who've dined at Shalom Japan over the years, thank you for coming in and wanting to experience a little bit of our passion and story. And of course our staff, past and present, who make the restaurant run. Thank you for your hard work. Especially Eryk Estevez. Your positivity is infectious.

From Aaron: I am extremely grateful to the amazing friends I have. Nate, Jay, Alex, Leor, Chad, and the many others, thank you for always lending a helping hand when I need it, or an ear when I need someone to talk to. Your brilliance inspires me.

To the many great teachers in my life who were so instrumental in shaping me as a young person. Karen, Carolee, Jeff, Barry, and so many more. Teachers are so incredibly important.

To some of the great chefs I've worked for and with over the years. Thank you for sharing your knowledge and passion. Thanks to Luke, for your continued mentorship, and to Tony, for giving some mostly self-taught kid out of art school a chance to cook in your kitchen.

To Sawa's parents, Kazumasa and Shuko Okochi. Thank you for welcoming me into your family and your home. I feel so grateful.

To my Grandma Helene, I wish you could have seen our book. You would have been so proud. And to my parents, thank you for your unconditional love and support and letting me mess up your kitchen all those times when I was younger. I'm sorry, but thank you. To my brother, for constantly asking me when dinner was going to be ready all those years ago, giving me a preview of my career path, and what it would be like to feel the pressure of trying to get food out to hungry people.

Thank you to those beautiful children of ours, Kaishu and Mayako. I hope when you are teenagers, you'll open this book and still think your dad is cool.

And lastly, thank you to Sawako, my co-everything. There is nobody else I'd rather be on this journey with. I'm so grateful we found each other.

From Sawa: To my mom, Shuko. You taught me without teaching me how to love food and the importance of nourishing your loved ones. To my dad, Kazumasa, for loving me and letting me do what I wanted to do. If you hadn't said go to the US, none of it would have happened.

To Aaron's family, Mindy and Howard, Grandma Helene, Heather, David, Arthur, Desi, and Hendrix. Thank you for welcoming me into your family with open arms.

To Kaishu, for having such a gentle soul and love for noodle and asparagus.

To Mayako, for your million-dollar smile and strong mind. I love you both with all my heart. In a way, this book is for you two, so that you don't have to call us when you want to prepare udon in your college dormitory kitchen.

To Chikako, for not only watching our children, but loving them like your own family.

To my mentor, Anita Lo, for all the teachings you gave me, and giving me a chance.

To my kitchen sisters, Nicole and Sohui, for all things big sisters do for a little sister.

To all the great chefs and cooks I've cooked with along the way, Jes, Lulu, and others, thank you for sharing your kitchen life with me.

To Takaki and Kaori, for help with translation.

To all of my friends, near and far, including the Aozora community, the Arbor community, and the grill community "Sukiyaki Friday" organizer Megu and everyone who comes to share Friday al fresco dinner, thank you for listening and supporting me throughout this journey. It takes a whole village of friends to raise children. Thank you.

Last but not least, Aaron, for being my co-author, co-owner, co-parent, and best husband and friend. Without you, I would have given up. I love you.

From Gabriella: This cookbook has been a long time in the making, longer than I care to admit! I am grateful to my collaborators, Aaron and Sawa, for persevering until we hit our goal of finding the right publisher for this beautiful book. Thank you Kelly Snowden, our editor at Ten Speed, my dream cookbook publisher, for believing in this project and for your confident yet gentle guidance. To Lizzie Allen, our talented designer: I feel blessed that *Love Japan* was in your capable hands. Yuki Sugiura, your photography has given this book an elegance that is a reflection of your loveliness. Suzie Myers, thank you for your impeccable styling and eagle eye on set. David Black and Sarah Smith, thank you for making this shidduch between me and my co-authors. To my agent, Angela Miller, thank you for lending an ear whenever I need one.

Thanks to my friends and cookbook authors extraordinaire Adeena Sussman, Raquel Pelzel, Darra Goldstein, Leah Koenig, Sarah Karnasiewicz, and Jeffrey Yoskowitz for advising me on matters ranging from recipe testing to contract negotiation. Knowing that I have such an amazing brain trust to lean on means more than I can say.

Writing is an anxiety-making career, and I couldn't have come this far without the invaluable support and sympathetic ear of my family. To my mother, Anna, who told me that my writing was a gift, and that I should do something with it. She would stay up with high-school me until the wee hours of the morning as I procrastinated and pushed to meet my deadlines, a habit I am still trying to shake! To my sister and confidante, Shulamit, who was my first husband, and my roommate when I started freelancing. For years, she was the first set of eyes on every article I submitted, and the one who joined me on restaurant reviews. Shulamit, even as I struggled to get a foothold, you always believed in me. To my father, Ed, who has only had praise for my writing, and never questioned my choice when I left a stable job (with health insurance) to pursue this unpredictable path. To Oded, Eitan, and Gaia, you're the most loving crew a doda could ask for. And to my husband and my love, Bernie, for being by my side during the years that I sweated through this book, and for cooking your way through several of its recipes, to the enjoyment of many.

The road that has led me here has been long, full of supportive friends, family, and wonderful colleagues. I am thanking just a few, but I love you all.

About the Authors

EILON PAZ

In addition to being the mother of two lovely children, **Sawako Okochi** is co-chef and owner of Shalom Japan in Brooklyn, New York, with her husband, Aaron Israel. Sawa has a vibrant culinary background rooted in her Japanese upbringing in Hiroshima. She has worked at some of the finest restaurants in New York City, including Chanterelle, Annisa, and The Good Fork. She produced the Otakara Supper Club, which was written about in the *New York Times*. She has also been featured in Women Chefs of New York and *The Jewish Cookbook*.

Aaron Israel is the co-chef and owner of Shalom Japan in Brooklyn, New York, along with his wife, Sawako Okochi. A native New Yorker, he attended art school at the Maryland Institute College of Art, simultaneously pursuing his passion for fine art and food. After graduating, he moved back to New York and cooked with some of the city's most acclaimed chefs. He has been featured in the *New York Times*, the *New Yorker*, *New York* magazine, and numerous other publications, as well as *The Jewish Cookbook*. He is the father of two amazing kids and enjoys doing ceramics in whatever small amount of spare time he has.

Gabriella Gershenson is a James Beard Award–nominated food journalist. She has been on staff at *Saveur*, *Rachael Ray Every Day*, and *Time Out New York*, and is currently an editor at *Wirecutter*. Her writing has appeared in many publications, including the *Wall Street Journal*, the *New York Times*, and *Food & Wine*. She is an editor of *The 100 Most Jewish Foods* (Artisan) and the IACP Award–winning *On the Hummus Route* (Magica). Gabriella splits her time between Manhattan and upstate New York with her husband, Bernie, and their dog, Achilles.

Index

Typefaces: Commercial Type's Portrait and
Pangram Pangram's Neue Montreal

Library of Congress Cataloging-in-Publication
Data is on file with the publisher.

Hardcover ISBN: 9781984860521
eBook ISBN: 9781984860538

Printed in China

Editor: Kelly Snowden
Editorial assistant: Zoey Brandt
Production editor: Mark McCauslin
Designer and art director: Lizzie Allen
Production designers: Mari Gill and Faith Hague
Illustrations pages 143 & 147: Nick Durig
Production manager: Dan Myers
Prepress color manager: Nick Patton
Food stylist: Lisa Masuda
Prop stylist: Suzie Myers
Copyeditor: Kate Slate
Proofreaders: Erica Rose and Eldes Tran
Indexer: Elizabeth Parson
Publicist: Natalie Yera
Marketer: Stephanie Davis

10 9 8 7 6 5 4 3 2 1

First Edition